PELOPONNESE

By the staff of Editions Berlitz

How to use our guide

- All the practical information, hints and tips that you will need before and during your trip start on page 102, with a complete rundown of contents on page 105.
- For general background, see the sections The Region and the People, p. 6, and A Brief History, p. 11.
- All the sights to see are listed between pages 27 and 88. Our own choice of sights most highly recommended is pinpointed by the Berlitz traveller symbol.
- Sports, entertainment and all other leisure activities are described between pages 89 and 95, while information on restaurants and cuisine is to be found on pages 96 to 101.
- Finally, there is an index at the back of the book, pp. 127–128.

Although we make every effort to ensure the accuracy of all the information in this book, changes occur incessantly. We cannot therefore take responsibility for facts, prices, addresses and circumstances in general that are constantly subject to alteration. Our guides are updated on a regular basis as we reprint, and we are always grateful to readers who let us know of any errors, changes or serious omissions they come across.

Text: Suzanne Patterson
Photography: Jacques Bétant
Layout: Doris Haldemann
We are particularly grateful to the Greek National Tourist Organization for their help in the preparation of this guide. We would also like to thank Mrs. Vanna Philippides, Theodore and Elaine Palashis and Dimitri Karalis for valuable assistance.
Cartography: Falk-Verlag, Hamburg

Contents

Cover photo: The village of Driópi in the Argolid region.

5

The Region and the People

The Peloponnese offers the greatest concentration of antique sites, glorious landscapes and sheer pleasure to be found in all Greece—or perhaps anywhere. Its tenuous link to the Attic mainland severed by a shipping canal across the Isthmus of Corinth, the region is now really a big island, shaped vaguely like a hand with three fingers and a thumb.

The scenery varies from sandy beaches and rocky promontories to silvery olive groves and craggy mountains, the highest often snow-capped. And the light is almost palpable as it flickers and refracts from rocks, rooftops, leaves and waves.

Typical scenes: neat white-washed houses, and Greeks of all ages in a friendly café.

In Frankish and Byzantine times the Peloponnese was called Morea, which means "mulberry" in Greek—perhaps due to its leaf-like shape. The present name, Pelopónnisos, comes from the mythical Pelops, who was served up as a dish for the gods by his father, Tantalos, and on whose descendants the outraged gods laid a terrible curse.

Here you'll find great names resonant of past splendours and tragedies: Mycenae, home of the cursed house of Atreus, where in legend Orestes murdered his mother in a palace decked with gold; Epidauros, the sylvan spa where the arts of healing were developed by Asklepios (Aesculapius), and site of the ancient outdoor theatre that remains a venue for Classical plays; Olympia, with ruins of temples and statues created at the height of Greece's Golden Age. Here in the 8th century B.C. were inaugurated the Olympic Games, the Pelo-

ponnese's great contribution to the peace of mankind.

The Peloponnese is also remembered as the cradle of the Mycenaean civilization, which rose to power about 1400 B.C. The ruins of its capital at Mycenae still stand—stark and awe-inspiring—and the delicate gold objects brought to light in excavations are now dazzling exhibits in the National Archaeological Museum in Athens. In the 5th century B.C., Sparta led the Greeks to victory over Xerxes' Persia, becoming paramount among Greek cities after the Peloponnesian War.

Later the Peloponnese was invaded and occupied by Romans and Slavs, Franks, Venetians and Turks. And like the other Greeks, the people of the Peloponnese learned to deal with the invaders by assimilating and civilizing them.

But the outsiders made their mark, too: the crusading Frankish knights built proud bastions and towers along the coast; the Byzantine despots erected exquisite churches and fortresses; and most important, Byzantium bequeathed its religion—the Orthodox faith—and much of its cultural heritage.

There's much to see besides ancient ruins. You can visit the old towns and fortresses of the Máni peninsula, making the charming port of Gíthio your base; or wander the fortified cities like Monemvasía. Náfplio (ancient Nauplia), one of Greece's prettiest towns, occupies its own peninsula, its venerable forts perched and brooding over the harbour, the shimmering bay a mesmerizing sight from dawn to dark.

Sports-minded visitors will revel in the miles of bathing beaches and tranquil sailing waters; hikers and climbers can spend a varied and rewarding holiday exploring the ruggedly beautiful hinterland.

The people themselves contribute to everyday enjoyment. Hospitality is spontaneous and well meant. Don't be surprised if a jeweller pulls out a bottle of *oúzo* or beer for you, even if you're "just looking", or if a shop assistant hands you a bag of fresh peaches. You or your children will often be given a special sweet after dinner, since the Greeks adore children, love to eat and delight in seeing others enjoy themselves at table.

The Greeks wisely consider work secondary to living in harmony with nature. The siesta hours are sensibly observed. So, do as the Greeks do

A fisherman on Hydra prepares his nets for the day's catch.

and take it easy in the afternoon, especially in summer.

In hotels and restaurants many people speak English, French or German. But even halting attempts at Greek will be appreciated, whether by an old lady tending chickens or a stone-worker restoring a house.

Tradition prevails. Greek men still sit around sipping coffee from morning to midnight, the older ones invariably toying with their worry beads. Wherever you go you'll hear music—not rock or pop, but quavery tunes in the Greek mode. There's also *bouzoúki* music, dancing and singing.

The Peloponnese offers little in the way of organized amusements. You'll do better to relax and appreciate the Peloponnese and its people for what they are —natural and unspoiled.

Pines, olive trees and cactus plants grow profusely in the Peloponnese.

A Brief History

The Peloponnese appears to have been inhabited in the 3rd millennium B.C. by a people of Asiatic descent, but their exact origins—even the language they spoke—remain the subject of conjecture.

From about 2000 B.C., wandering bands from western Russia or Asia Minor filtered into Attica and other parts of Greece. Known as the Achaeans, they were the first Greek-speaking people to reach the peninsula. Over the centuries they developed the rich My-

Facts and Figures

Although much of the information given below can be found in various sections of our guide, key facts are grouped here for a quick briefing.

Geography: The Peloponnese comprises seven prefectures *(nómos)*: Korinthía, Achaía, Ílis, Arkadía, Messinía, Lakonía and Argolís. The peninsula extends southwards from the narrow Isthmus of Corinth, once the fragile link to the Attic mainland and now severed by a canal 75 feet (23 m.) wide. The area of the Peloponnese is 21,439 square kilometres (8,275 sq. mi.).

Population: 1,005,000

Chief cities: Pátra (pop. 141,000); Kalamáta (pop. 42,000); Corinth (pop. 22,500); Pírgos (pop. 22,000).

Government: Republic. Multi-party parliamentary system. The seven prefectures are administered by local governors; each is represented in Parliament by deputies, the number depending on the population of the district.

Religion: Ninety-six per cent of Greeks belong to the Orthodox Church, headed by the Patriarch of Constantinople and Archbishop of Athens.

Getting around: You can travel by plane, train, ferry, hydrofoil, bus, car or taxi, depending on where you are. A hired car is the most convenient means of transport. Taxis are plentiful and inexpensive. There are ferry connections to Athens and the Saronic Islands, among others.

cenaean civilization centred on the towns of Mycenae, Argos, Pylos (Pílos) and Tiryns in the Peloponnese.

The Achaeans' main rivals, and mentors, were the dazzling Minoans of Crete—that is, until about 1400 B.C., when the Minoan empire was devastated, probably by a volcanic eruption or an earthquake.

For the next several centuries the Mycenaeans dominated the Aegean and western Mediterranean. They were remarkable for their political organization, military strongholds and works of art. They practised their religion in temples and grottoes and buried their dead in circular "beehive" tombs that show a grandiose preoccupation with the after life. But a long series of conflicts—including the legendary siege of Troy under Agamemnon of Mycenae around 1200 B.C.— weakened these mighty mainland warriors.

Shortly before 1100 B.C. waves of Dorians from the north swept into the area on horseback. With iron spears and shields, they overwhelmed the Bronze Age chariots of Mycenae and broke down the Peloponnesian bastions. With the occupation of most of Greece by the Dorians, the unity of the Aegean world was destroyed and the peoples of Greece lost contact with the outside world and with each other. The ensuing "dark ages" lasted about three centuries; the arts languished, especially in Attica, though some geometric pottery was created.

The Rise of the City-State

After 900 B.C. a reawakening was under way. The Greeks invented their own alphabet, Homer composed his great work, *The Iliad,* immortalizing the Trojan War, and the reinstitution of commerce and cultural interchange helped bring new enlightenment. The 9th century B.C. saw the emergence of the city-state, which was to remain the geo-political force of Greek society for over a thousand years. The Greek world had fragmented into several hundred of these minirepublics, each enjoying complete autonomy. In the Peloponnese the most powerful included Sparta, Corinth and Argos.

Though they warred as often as they allied with each other, **13**

Handsome but headless, two lionesses top the massive gateway to the ruins of Mycenae.

This way to the Olympic Games: only judges and athletes were allowed to enter here.

Athenians, Spartans, Thebans and others shared a sense of national identity. They were all Greeks, calling their country Hellas (Graecia was the Roman name for the area); they had a common language and an evolving pan-Hellenic religion. In addition, the institution of official games at Olympia in 776 B.C. called for a truce in hostilities every four years, while athletes from the Peloponnese and later from all over Greece competed. Similar events at Delphi and Isthmia also played their part in bringing the Greeks together at regular intervals.

By 700 B.C., at the beginning of the so-called Archaic period, a recognizably Hellenic culture had developed. The Greeks were setting up colonies all over the Mediterranean and Black Sea regions, and agriculture and commerce were evolving. As the Greek monarchies waned, tyrants or "law-givers" emerged as champions of the yeomen against the nobles. During this time, the

Corinthian tyranny was the most powerful and the Isthmus of Corinth the hub of the Greek world.

It was not long before the tyrannies gave way to democracies in Athens and elsewhere. But Sparta, the rival to Athens, developed into a cruelly professional military state, characterized by infanticide and the harsh training of its soldier-citizens (see p. 73).

The Persian Wars

Persian expansion in the 6th century B.C. threatened the rise of Hellenism. The Persians' far-flung dominions included Greek settlements on the coast of present-day Turkey. When the Greek towns attempted a revolt in 499 B.C., Athens came to their assistance. In retaliation, King Darius of Persia set about incorporating the Greek mainland into his empire. In 490 B.C. he confidently launched an invasion of Attica. His forces and resources were vastly superior, but Darius hadn't reckoned with the amazing courage of the Greeks and their skill on the battlefield; Persian forces were roundly defeated on the Plain of Marathon.

When Darius died in 486 B.C., his son Xerxes vowed to achieve what his father could not and arrived in great strength by land and sea six years later. A few heroic troops under King Leonidas of Sparta held up the enormous Persian army at the pass of Thermopylae just long enough for Athens to be evacuated. As the Spartans gave way, Xerxes' army swept into Athens, destroying all the wooden structures on the Acropolis and plundering the city.

But defeat for the Persians lay round the corner. From his vantage point on a hill, Xerxes

saw his fleet of 700 ships enticed into the narrows of the Bay of Salamis by Themistocles' much smaller naval force and trounced. A decisive Greek victory over the Persians followed at Plataea in 479 B.C. Greek independence had been preserved and with it the foundations of Western civilization. In 478 B.C. the islands and cities of the Aegean formed the Delian League, centred on Delos, to oppose any further invasion by the Persians. The Peloponnesians, who were excluded from the alliance, formed their own league.

The Peloponnesian War

While Sparta was divided by internal problems, Athens emerged as leader of the Delian League, transforming it more or less into an empire; its "subject allies" were obliged to pay a tribute of money, and attempts at secession were repressed with force.

Under Perikles, an aristocrat with liberal ideas who was in effect the supreme ruler of Athens and its empire for 30 years, Greece knew a time of unprecedented greatness. Literature and the arts, philosophy and science flourished; temples and shrines were put up, culminating in the construction of the **16** Parthenon, Erechtheion and Theseum in Athens, the Temple of Zeus at Olympia, the temple at Bassae and the great temple at Delphi. This cultural flowering was followed in the 4th century B.C. by the building of the immense theatre and gymnasium at Epidauros and the Leonidaeum at Olympia. The period is known as Greece's Golden Age.

But Sparta and dissatisfied members of the Delian League resented Athens' prosperity and refused to co-operate. Such intense economic and ideological rivalry eventually led to war between the two most powerful city-states, Athens and Sparta; the other city-states took part sporadically.

For 27 years the Peloponnesian War (431–404 B.C.) dragged on, a conflict which proved debilitating for all concerned. Finally Sparta, with naval help from former foe Persia, cut off Athens' vital corn supply by blockade and victory was secured. Athens was obliged to destroy its fortifications and Sparta took over the leadership of the Delian League, instituting a harsh regime. In 386 B.C. the Spartans signed the Treaty of Antalcidas, by which the Persians promised to continue their support of Sparta in return for a free hand in Asia.

Subjugation and Empire

As periodic struggles between the city-states continued, in the north the star of King Philip II of Macedonia was in the ascendant. Taking advantage of the weakness caused by years of warring, Philip quickly brought the whole of Greece to submission. Athens resisted bitterly, spurred on by the master orator Demosthenes, whose hatred of Philip inspired the tirades known as the *Philippics*. But the Battle of Chaeronea in 338 B.C. proved a decisive victory for the Macedonian king. At a pan-Hellenic congress in Corinth, Philip declared a federation of Greek states with himself at its head, wielding almost dictatorial powers. His first aim was to wage a new campaign against the Persians, although many of the Greeks were unwilling to participate.

Before he could move against the enemy, Philip was assassinated in 336 B.C. But his son Alexander was to earn the epithet "the Great" for his subjugation of countries all over the Near East, forming an unprecedented empire. Alexander gained power in Macedonia itself by executing other claimants to the throne. He marched on into Greece, razing Thebes and cowing other Greek cities, which were busy passing votes of thanks to Philip's assassins. Then in 334 B.C. he had himself "elected" leader and crossed into Asia Minor with 40,000 men at his back. He swept through Egypt and across Persia to India, founding at least 30 towns bearing his name. When he realized that there were no more lands to conquer, Alexander is said to have sat down and wept. He died of fever in 323 B.C. at the age of only 33. In his short life he had united Macedonia, Greece and Persia and carried the Greek language and culture to three continents.

After Alexander's death, confusion reigned for many years. None of the Macedonian generals who survived him were strong enough to hold the far-flung empire together and it was divided into several kingdoms. The Greek city-states formed an uneasy alliance, but their inability to maintain peace among themselves led to a general decline.

Nevertheless, philosophy and the arts continued to thrive. Stoicism and Epicureanism, both of which evolved in Athens at this time, emphasized wisdom as detachment from the vagaries of troubled times. During this period the focus of culture shifted from mainland Greece to Asia Minor.

Romans in Greece

While Macedonia itself was weakened by wars and internal quarrels, the Roman state was expanding abroad. The defeat of the Macedonian King Perseus at Pydna in 168 B.C. brought to an end both a long succession of wars and the Macedonian empire. In 148 B.C. Macedonia became a Roman province, along with the rest of Greece. Harsh treatment by the Romans inspired a revolt by the Achaean League, a federation of cities in the north Peloponnese originally established to overthrow the Macedonian rulers. In reprisal the Roman general Mummius sacked Corinth in 146 B.C. and its inhabitants were sold as slaves.

But the Greeks achieved a far more subtle conquest over the Romans—a cultural one. As Rome borrowed liberally from the Greeks in styles of literature, architecture and sculpture, a progressive Hellenization took place among the Romans. Thus Greece "civilized" militaristic Rome, and in this way handed down its culture to all of Europe. In the words of the Latin poet Horace: "Captive Greece made captive her rude conqueror".

In 44 B.C. Julius Caesar founded a new colony on the site of the old town of Corinth. This city quickly became a bustling commercial centre. It was also known for its citizens' promiscuous and pleasure-loving conduct, a state of affairs which prompted the Apostle Paul, while in Greece (51–52 A.D.), to write his reproving Epistles to the Corinthians.

In the period known as the Pax Romana (31 B.C. to A.D. 330), Greece was especially favoured. Athens became an important university centre for Rome, and young Romans were sent there to acquire learning and culture. The Achaean League was revived, separating Greece from Macedonia.

No Roman loved Greece more than Nero, who thought the Greeks the only audience worthy of his talents. Nero won chariot races nct only at the Isthmian Games in Corinth but also in Olympia in A.D. 67. (The eccentric emperor was apparently allowed to win.) He also walked off with the prizes in the singing competition, introduced for his own benefit.

Under Byzantine Rule

Incursions into Greece by northern tribes began in the 2nd century A.D. The vast Roman Empire had grown unwieldy and difficult to rule, so Diocletian divided it into a western and eastern half, ruling from the east rather than Rome. Constantine reunited the two and established a new capital at Byzantium in A.D. 330, renaming it Constantinople.

The Emperor Theodosius disapproved of the pagan aspects of the Delphian and Olympic Games and ordered them to be halted by a famous edict in 393. On the death of Theodosius two years later, the empire was

Byzantine culture and art are part of the Greek heritage: an icon of the Virgin and Child at Méga Spíleo.

divided again. Greek in culture and ideas, Constantinople became the Christian capital of the Eastern, or Byzantine, Empire.

From about 440 on, Greece was pillaged by Goths, Huns and Vandals. The Western Empire collapsed under the strain of barbarian invasions in 476, a date that conveniently divides the ancient from the medieval world; but the Eastern Empire continued to play a significant role amid the changing political geography. As Constantinople became the centre of power, Greece fell further into decline. In 529 Justinian closed the Athens Academy, and Latin gradually superseded Greek as the language of the empire. Byzantine-style Christianity took precedence over the polytheistic religions of the Greeks and Romans, except in the mountain regions of Lakonia in the Peloponnese, always known for its independent ways. (The people here did not adopt Christianity until the 9th century.)

In the latter part of the 6th century, Slav raids grew in intensity and their impact was felt throughout Greece. In 746 a plague transmitted from the Near East broke out in Monemvasia in the Peloponnese and subsequently ravaged the whole empire. Greece lost thousands

in the scourge, and as skilled workers sought employment in Constantinople, the Slavs moved in to fill the gaps and in most places were soon assimilated.

Early in the 9th century, with Greece under threat from Saracens (nomadic Arab tribes) and Bulgars, the Slavs of the Peloponnese rose in revolt against Byzantine rule, attacking the fortress of Patra. The rebellion was put down, as was another in 841.

Advent of the Franks

In spite of Greek objection to taxes levied by Byzantium, all remained relatively peaceful in the empire—until the Norman conquerors of southern Italy came seeking to match the exploits of their compatriot William the Conqueror in England. In 1146, Roger II of Sicily and his Norman warriors landed at Itea (Gulf of Corinth) and marched on Thebes; they plundered the city before continuing to Corinth, looting it as well

The Boúrdzi Tower in Methóni, once a proud Turkish fortress.

before sailing home with the spoils. In 1185 they again invaded Greek soil, but were defeated at Salonica.

After the sack of Constantinople by the leaders of the Fourth Crusade in 1204, the Byzantine Empire was divided between western rulers. Guillaume de Champlitte and Geoffroi de Villehardouin, two **21**

French feudal lords, agreed to bring the Peloponnese under their own control, a bargain sanctioned by Boniface de Montferrat, who had quickly taken possession of Salonica. Champlitte and Villehardouin, with a force of a mere 200 men, won most of the Peloponnese and divided it into 12 Frankish baronies. Champlitte died in 1209 on the return journey to France, and Villehardouin became Prince of Achaea, the official title of the Frankish principality of the Peloponnese, which was also known then as Morea.

Meanwhile Venice had emerged as a formidable maritime power, gaining control over the Peloponnese ports of Modon and Coron. Monemvasia remained the sole bastion of Byzantine forces. The latter was finally taken by the Franks with Venice's help in 1249 after a three-year siege.

With them the Franks brought a touch of their homeland—an elegant court life, music and dancing. They also built a huge fortress at Mistra, several castles at Killini, the fortified cities around the Mani and some Gothic chapels.

Guillaume III de Villehardouin was captured by Byzantine forces in 1262, but was allowed freedom in exchange for the fortress at Monemvasia, Mistra and the Mani. The acquisition of this territory heralded the restoration of Byzantine authority in the Peloponnese. Until 1282 Michael Paleologos, Emperor of Byzantium, ruled from the Peloponnese, using Mistra and Killini as headquarters. He and his Paleologos successors were known as the Despots of Mistra.

Guillaume III's only child, Isabella, married successively the son of Charles I of Naples, a Flemish nobleman and a prince of the House of Savoy, bringing the succession into dispute after her death. A band of mercenaries, the Navarese Company, took advantage of the confusion and occupied the peninsula in 1383.

Turks and Venetians
Although Byzantine power was on the decline, the empire managed to retain control of the Peloponnese until 1443. But the Turks and the Venetians were busy, too. The Venetians had taken Argos (1388), Nauplia (1388) and Lepanto (1407), while the Ottoman Turks made inroads into Macedonia. Byzantium itself fell to the Turks in 1453. Instead of uniting in the face of disaster, the Byzantines still holding out in the Peloponnese quarrelled among

themselves, disputes which were exploited by the Turks to their own advantage.

By 1461 the Turks had occupied the whole of the Peloponnese, except for a few ports still under Venetian control. By 1540 even these had fallen to the Turks.

In 1571 a Christian coalition, the Holy League, which included the Papacy, Venice, Spain, Genoa, Savoy and the Knights of Malta, defeated the Turks in a big naval battle near Lepanto, across the Gulf of Corinth from the Peloponnese (near today's Patra). But the victory brought little relief to Greece. Mountain rebels in the Mani rose up against Turkish rule to no avail.

While the Turks were busy fighting at the gates of Vienna, the Venetians stepped in to assert authority in the Peloponnese. By the time the Venetians had quelled further unrest in the Mani, the whole of the Peloponnese had degenerated into chaos.

Meanwhile, the population of the Peloponnese had been greatly reduced by starvation and poverty. The Venetians attempted to redress the balance through management of agriculture and by immigration from northern Greece, but although these measures brought relative prosperity, the Venetians did not win the hearts of the Peloponnesians. In 1715 the Turks overran the Peloponnese again and in 1718 Venice finally relinquished control.

The decline of the Ottoman Empire gave impetus to Russian expansion in the Black Sea region. Championing the Greek cause, the Russians attempted further to erode Ottoman power, leading to the Russo-Turkish war and culminating in defeat for the Russians in 1774.

During the early years of the peace which followed, both Greeks and Turks were attacked by marauding bands of Albanians, who created havoc far and wide, from the Peloponnese north over the Isthmus. A plague (1781–85) further decimated the population, but thereafter conditions began to improve.

Towards Independence

The Greeks hated Turkish rule for its inefficiency, corruption and brutality. Nationalist sentiments were strong and insurrection was in the air, especially in the Peloponnese, where the *kléftes,* part brigands, part patriots, had become more daring than ever.

The year 1821 marks the start of the Greek War of Independ- **23** ence. On March 25, a spontaneous and badly co-ordinated rebellion began at the Monastery of Agía Lávra near Kalávrita in the Peloponnese. Clergy, landowners and magistrates joined forces behind the Archbishop of Pátra, who had raised the standard against the Turks—and the infidels were then massacred *en masse*.

The Turks responded with retaliatory massacres of Greeks in Macedonia and Constantinople, where the Patriarch was hanged on Easter Sunday. Early in 1825 Ibrahim Pasha, son of the Egyptian leader Muhammad Ali, landed an army of more than 10,000, securing large chunks of the Peloponnese. Missolonghi, just across the Isthmus, was taken in 1826. It was here that the poet Byron died in 1824 after coming to Greece to fight for the cause of independence.

In 1827 Count Ioannis Capodistria (former secretary to Tsar Alexander I of Russia) was elected the first President of Greece, and the capital of the provisional government was set up at Náfplio (Nauplia).

That same year, the anxious allied European powers—Britain, France and Russia—intervened and managed to trap and totally destroy the Egypto-Turkish fleet at Navarino. Although many Greeks were still under Turkish rule, the new state was guaranteed its independence by the three European powers at the Conference of London in 1830.

However, the *kléftes* were not happy with the arrangements and assassinated Capodistria in 1831. Following the directives of the Conference of London, Greece became a monarchy under Otto of Bavaria. The Turkish sultan recognized Greek independence in 1832.

Modern Times

Twentieth-century Greek history has been as chaotic as any since the days of the ancients. The dominant figure between 1910 and 1935 was Eleftherios Venizelos, a Cretan politician who was several times prime minister of Greece. Under his leadership, Greece joined the Allies against the Germans in 1917.

From 1936 to 1940 Greece fell under the military dictatorship of Ioannis Metaxas, while the king, George II, remained titular head.

In World War II the Greeks put up a valiant resistance to the Italians and Germans, who invaded and occupied most of the country. The people suffered terrible hardships until they were liberated by the Allies in 1944. But liberation brought to a head the rivalries of guerrilla bands—communist and royalist—and the country was torn by internal strife. The fierce battles amounted to civil war in the years between 1945 and 1949, ending with defeat for the communists.

In recent times, Greece has seen several changes of government. In 1967 King Constantine went into exile after a junta of colonels came to power. The junta conducted a repressive regime until 1974, when it collapsed after the Turkish invasion of Cyprus. A former conservative prime minister, Constantine Karamanlis, returned from exile as head of government.

In January 1981, Greece joined the European Economic Community; later in the year elections brought a socialist government to power, the first in the history of the country. Many banks and businesses were nationalized, accounting for some 30 per cent of Greek industry. During the post-war period, tourism has become Greece's biggest industry, bringing in millions of dollars annually.

Going home means just a few steps down a sunny street.

Historical Landmarks

B.C.

c.1400–1200	Mycenaean civilization.
c.1200	Trojan War.
c.1100	Dorians come in from north. Dark Ages.
c.1000	Rise of Greek city-states.
776	Olympic Games instituted at Olympia.
490	King Darius of Persia invades Attica.
480	Xerxes invades Greece and plunders Athens.
479	Greeks win victory over Persians at Plataea.
478	Formation of Delian League.
460–429	Perikles comes to power in Athens.
431–404	Peloponnesian War. Sparta triumphs over Athens.
359	Philip II becomes King of Macedonia.
338	Philip beats Greeks at Chaeronea.
336	Alexander the Great succeeds Philip.
334–324	Alexander's epic march of conquest.
148	Macedonia and Greece become a Roman province.
146	Romans sack Corinth.
44	Julius Caesar founds new colony at Corinth.

A.D.

395	Roman Empire divided.
476	Collapse of Western Empire.
1204	Geoffroi de Villehardouin conquers Peloponnese.
1453	Byzantium falls to the Ottoman Turks.
1461	Turks occupy most of Peloponnese.
1821	Greek War of Independence begins.
1827	Capodistria elected first President of Greece.
1832	Turkish sultan recognizes Greek independence.
1917	Greece joins Allies in World War I.
1941	Greece invaded by Italians and then Germans.
1944	Greece liberated by Allies.
1945–1949	Civil war between royalists and communists.
1967	Junta of colonels comes to power.
1974	Democratic government is restored.
1981	Greece joins European Economic Community.

Where to Go

There is no perfect way to travel around the Peloponnese. Visitors who drive themselves usually come from Athens on the motorway that goes through Corinth and west to Pátra. The first sightseeing stop after crossing the canal would therefore be Corinth and its ancient city. From here we suggest you head south to Náfplio, an attractive seaside town and an excellent base for tours to the major sites of antiquity on the Argolid peninsula.

From Náfplio you can return to the north coast for an excursion up into the Vouraikós River valley, continuing on through Pátra to Killíni in the west. You bear inland to reach Olympia—not to be missed. From here the itinerary runs south to Pílos, Methóni, Sparta, Mistra, the Máni and Monemvasía.

It's up to each individual traveller to plan his route according to preference. There is always a choice, depending on time, season and weather. The order used in this guide is simply a rough indication and should be adapted to circumstances.

Words of Wisdom About Walking

There's nothing like a tour of the Peloponnese to put you in good physical shape, especially if you plan to visit the archaeological sites, some of which are perched high on rocky hills. These are some places where walking may be wearying to arduous:

Mycenae is deceptive; the hill is not strikingly high, but it can seem a long haul to the top of the ruins. Acrocorinth is daunting on a hot day. The last third of the climb consists of rough paths more suitable for goats than human beings; the first part is rocky, but not too difficult. Mistra's hillside location also requires strength for walking, climbing or scrambling, although you can choose between several routes. Much of ancient Monemvasía's glory lies way uphill, but the steep climb is comparatively short, and the glorious scenery may also be appreciated from the lower town.

In all cases be sure to take sturdy walking or hiking shoes that don't slip on stones. High-heeled shoes are definitely not recommended. In summer wear light cotton clothing, a hat and sunglasses, and try to avoid the hottest hours of the day from noon to 4 p.m.

THE PELOPONNESE

Corinth and the Isthmus

Approaching Corinth from Athens you traverse the narrow strip of land that once linked the peninsula to the mainland. The Isthmus has now been severed by the **Corinth Canal,** which transformed the peninsula into a big island and provided a waterway between the Ionian and Aegean seas.

The 6½-kilometre-long trough of the canal looks like a straight narrow ribbon. It has been cut out of variegated layers of rock from different geological eras, which give the walls a striped effect.

The canal has had a chequered history. Attempts to cut one have been made since the 7th or 6th century B.C., when Periander, Tyrant of Corinth, tried and failed. The Roman

---

It's Greek to Me

Finding your way around in the Peloponnese will be much easier if you learn the Greek Alphabet. This isn't as difficult as it sounds. All street signs and some road indications are written in capital letters—many of which are already familiar to you. See ALPHABET on page 106 for a quick course in reading Greek.

In this book we have used time-honoured English spellings for well-known places like Corinth, Olympia and Sparta, while indicating their modern Greek names in parentheses. Elsewhere we have given the transcriptions of the Greek names as the most useful means of asking your way.

The transcription system used in Greece itself is in a state of virtual chaos, and you'll find, for example,

Ágios, Hágios, Ájos, Áyos and *Ághios (meaning Saint)* indifferently.

Stress, a very important feature of the Greek language, is indicated by an accent mark (´) over the vowel of the syllable to be emphasized.

Two words you'll want to learn immediately are ΠΛΑΤΕΙΑ *(platía),* meaning square, and ΟΔΟΣ *(odós),* street, which are often omitted in addresses. Here are translations of some other Greek words:

Agía	⎫
Ágii	⎬ Saint(s), Holy
Ágios	⎪
Ósios	⎭
Kólpos	Gulf
Leofóros	Avenue
Límni	Lake
Óros	Mountain
Panagía	Our Lady
Profítis	Prophet
Tachidromío	Post Office

Emperor Nero also ordered a canal to be dug and even took a turn at hacking at the rock himself with a golden shovel—to no avail. Meanwhile ships wishing to take the "short cut" over the Isthmus were hauled by cart over a rocky road called a *diolkos,* which you can still see on the mainland side.

Others kept digging sporadically, but after A.D. 68 nobody made any further tries until a French company started work in 1882. Misfortune dogged even this attempt: the firm went bankrupt, leaving the work to be completed by the Greeks themselves in 1893.

A turn off after the bridge over the canal brings you to ancient **Isthmia,** the site of the Sanctuary of Poseidon. On the road from Athens, you pass sections of the **Isthmian Wall,** which at one time extended 10

Ships can take a short cut through the Corinth Canal.

kilometres across the Isthmus. Just before you reach the sanctuary, you see the best-preserved traces of the wall, 23 feet (7 m.) high and 8 feet (2½ m.) thick. Isthmia was also the venue of games that ranked on a par with those in Olympia. Held bi-annually, but in between the Olympics, the Isthmian Games attracted athletes from all over Greece; winners were crowned with parsley instead of the Olympic wild olive.

The **museum** on the sanctuary grounds displays athletic equipment, accompanied by details about the games and clear explanations in English. Other important archaeological finds from the site include two enormous lustral basins from the 5th century B.C. and fragments of large mural decorations from the nearby seaport of Kenchreai *(Kechrié)*. Museum charts help you to find your way round the **ruins** outside, where traces remain of the sanctuary, a theatre, and early and later stadiums.

New Corinth *(Kórinthos)* looks like what it is—a city hastily reconstructed several times after earthquakes. There's not much of interest to the tourist in the modern town, but being moderately large, it does offer plenty of shops and a few restaurants.

ANCIENT CORINTH

Ancient Corinth

Once a wealthy, pleasure-loving town—"sin city" to the ancient world—old Corinth uncovers for you layers of long gone history. This was a teeming and populous city occupying a plateau overlooking the sea, under the towering rocky citadel of Acrocorinth, and commanding a strategic position between Attica and the Peloponnese.

In the Archaic period, Corinth was already a prosperous centre, becoming even richer and more powerful under the Tyrant Periander (627–586 B.C.), who demanded that Egypt, Phoenicia, Arabia and Carthage, among others, pay high fees to use the Isthmus road for carting their ships between the Ionian and Aegean seas.

The Corinthians produced and sold vases and other pottery, and excelled at constructing seaworthy ships; they designed the first trireme, a galley with three banks of oars that became crucial to warfare in ancient times. In the 5th century B.C., the architectural style of Corinth, noted for its elaborate pediments and flowering column capitals, began to have a lasting influence throughout Greece.

Corinth founded colonies such as Korkyra (Corfu) and Syracuse. The city began to take precedence over Athens in the 4th century B.C., heading the League of Corinth, a coalition of Greek city-states headed first by Philip II and later by Alexander the Great.

From the 4th to the 2nd centuries B.C., Corinth revelled in great luxury—with banquets, music and attendant prostitution, as "priestesses" went about their business of seduction in the temple of Aphrodite.

In 146 B.C. the Roman consul Mummius laid Corinth to waste. Julius Caesar reconstructed the city in 44 B.C., naming it Colonia Laus Julia Corinthiensis; populated largely by freed slaves and Jews, it regained much of its former glory—and dissipated ways. St. Paul spent two years in Corinth working as a tentmaker and evangelizing on the side. Horrified by the prevailing lax morals, he was inspired to write the Epistles to the Corinthians.

After several barbarian invasions and earthquakes in the Middle Ages, Ancient Corinth was destroyed forever, leaving only the ruins you see today.

Just outside the entry to the site of Ancient Corinth lie the ruins of the *odeion,* a small Roman theatre, and behind it a **33** larger theatre, which reputedly seated 18,000 for gladiatorial contests, swimming competitions and other shows.

Inside the enclosure, your first stop might be the **museum,** endowed in 1931 by an American, Mrs. Ada Small Moore. One gallery exhibits dozens of charming Archaic ceramics of the type Corinth exported in the 7th century B.C. Another displays a remarkable head of Nero, among sculptures from the Greek and Roman periods, plus some striking mosaics of flowers, centaurs and animals.

Leaving the museum, you take some steps down to the Agora or marketplace. The most salient feature here is the 6th-century B.C. **Temple of Apollo,** commanding a magnificent view over the Gulf of Corinth, with seven of the original group of 38 monolithic columns still standing. On your way to the temple ruins, you pass the Sanctuary of Hera and a fountain to the mythological Glauke—second wife to Jason who sought the Golden Fleece.

The **Agora** itself comprises the ruins of a series of shops; the one in the centre still has its original barrel-vaulted appearance. At the far end of the Agora you reach the beginning of the **Lechaion,** or Royal Road, which leads down to the sea.

The well-preserved **Lower Peirene Fountain** nearby consists of arched chambers on several levels around a rectangular pond. Built and rebuilt over several periods, the fountain retains a Greek section in the atrium. Most of the colonnades and arcades are from the Roman period.

Acrocorinth

A jarringly rough—but passable —dirt road leads 3½ kilometres to the base of Acrocorinth, and from here it is a long haul on foot, at least an hour over steep and rocky terrain to the summit at 1,885 feet (575 m.).

Serving first as an acropolis to the Greeks, and centuries later as a Roman and then Byzantine fortress, the citadel fell to the Franks in 1210 after a five-year siege. It changed hands several times, from Italians and Mistra Despots to the Knights of Rhodes, and was dominated by the Venetians from 1687 to 1715, after which it went to the Turks.

Three imposing **gateways** mark the upward path, which

Outstanding in old Corinth: the Temple of Apollo and geometric Greco-Roman mosaics.

begins with a series of small barrack-like buildings. It's not far to the first portal in 14th-century Turkish style. From the upper two gateways you gain sweeping views to the sea and over rolling countryside. The third portal is flanked by two towers; one dates from the 4th century B.C., the other, in Byzantine style, is from a later date. The open expanse behind was the Turkish quarter; you'll be able to identify the ruins of a small mosque. At this point,

weary walkers can turn back without feeling too guilty.

Beyond the third gate, if you decide to persevere, lies a jumble of ruins: minarets, cisterns carved out of the rock and Greek chapels. A **keep** dominating a 13th-century Frankish stronghold built by Guillaume de Villehardouin affords a fine view of Byzantine ramparts with their rectangular towers.

Retracing your steps, you can take a choice of two paths: one leads to the **Upper Peirene**

Fountain, with a Hellenistic subterranean chamber, the vaults rebuilt by the Romans. Below this a spring once flowed; according to mythology, it gushed water after being kicked by the winged horse Pegasus.

The other fork of the path leads to the Temple of Aphrodite, crowning the summit of Acrocorinth. From here you have a fabulous panoramic **view** of the Isthmus all the way out to the Bay of Corinth.

The Argolid

The scenic city of Náfplio is the perfect base for touring the whole Argolid region, which includes outstanding archaeological sites such as Epidauros, Mycenae, Tiryns and Argos.

Tobacco is grown in the Argolid. The region also boasts sandy strands like this crescent (below) at Karathóna.

✦ Náfplio

Formerly known as Nauplia, Náfplio is one of the most attractive spots in Greece. The largest city in the region, home to 10,500 inhabitants, it is situated on a rocky peninsula overlooking a large bay, crowned by the imposing Venetian Fort Palamídi. The spectacular views, the intriguing corners and byways of the old town, and a wide choice of hotels and restaurants make Náfplio a favourite stop for visitors to the Peloponnese.

There may have been a big Mycenaean naval settlement here 3,000 years ago, but little evidence of this remains. The legendary founder was Nauplios, son of the sea god Poseidon; one of his descendants, Palamedes, has been credited with inventing most of the Greek alphabet, weights and measures, dice games and chess.

Náfplio did not enter recorded history until about A.D. 1210, when it was taken from Byzantium by the Franks and awarded to Othon de la Roche by his fellow crusader Geoffroi de Villehardouin. It seesawed back and forth between Franks, Venetians and Turks until rebellious Greeks under the formidable woman admiral Bouboulina took the supposedly impregnable fortress and ousted the Turks in November 1822.

In 1828 the first President of Greece, Count Ioannis Capodistria, formed his government here. But dissension arose, and Capodistria was assassinated by disgruntled former revolutionaries from the Máni. His successor, Otto of Bavaria, moved the government to Athens in 1834, but left behind a legacy of handsome Neoclassical buildings.

Síntagma Square (Constitution Square) in the centre of the old town is an ideal starting point for a tour of the city. The square is attractive, clean and airy, surrounded by shops and tavernas galore and framed by old golden façades. On one side sits an endearing Venetian statue of a lion (more pussycat than lion); behind it a former mosque served briefly as the first parliament of independent Greece and is now used as a meeting place and cinema.

The **museum,** built as a naval arsenal by the Venetians in 1713, stands out as the most striking building on the square, with its arcades in golden stone. The most interesting exhibits on the main floor are: a suit of Mycenaean armour found near Déndra (about 11 km. from Argos) in 1960; a very ancient

Kids while away the time in Náfplio.

stele with bas-reliefs; gold jewellery and grotesque idol heads. Besides votive objects and pottery, the second floor displays a Hellenistic terracotta bath.

Exploring the small streets nearby, you'll see several churches. The Ágios Geórgios cathedral, constructed in the 16th century in mainly Byzantine style, contains King Otto's throne. Ágios Spirídonas, a little Venetian-style church and monastery, was the site of the assassination of Capodistria on September 27, 1831.

In Ipsilántou Street, about two blocks from Síntagma towards the port, is the attractive **Peloponnesian Folklore Foundation,** with excellent displays on the making of Greek fabrics in ancient and modern times and other exhibits of stunning regional costumes and jewellery. Founded in 1974 in a restored 18th-century mansion, the privately supported museum has a well-stocked gift shop across the cool courtyard.

The **waterfront** is a pleasant place to linger, since the harbour scene is always arresting. The fort out in the bay is the fortified islet of **Boúrdzi,** built by the Venetians in 1471 and modified a few times since. It served as a prison and hangman's home, and for a brief time in recent years as a tourist hostel. It is now deserted, but small boats can be hired for the short trip over to look around.

Near the waterfront and City Hall is a monument dedicated in 1903 to French military personnel killed in the Greek War of Independence. You can walk right around the peninsula from Aktí Miaoúli, the quay named after a famous Greek revolutionary general. Here you'll be tempted to stop in dozens of lively shops and tavernas. If you forge on past them, you'll eventually round

the peninsula, finding on the other side a gorgeous pine-clad landscape, with good bathing from the rocks at **Arvanitiá Beach.**

Fort Palamídi tops the summit of a formidable rocky peak 705 feet (215 m.) high, commanding a majestic view of Náfplio, its bay and the whole of the Argolid. In the old days intrepid tourists had to struggle up over 800 steps to visit the fort, but today a wide, paved road makes access easy for cars and buses. Built during the Venetian occupation, between 1711 and 1714, the fortress complex is entered through several grand gateways bearing the Lion of St. Mark. Impressive ramparts surround the fortress courtyards and former barracks. The view from up here is awesome—a dark, ultramarine sea lies far below, and forceful winds often whistle round the craggy peak.

Take the right-hand fork of the paved road leading downhill to the long, sandy **Karathóna Beach.** Wild and usually breezy, this beach offers the advantage of bathing in near solitude. Grab a snack of fresh fish and salad at the quaint little taverna here.

Akronáfplio is not so exalted as Palamídi, but it also towers conspicuously over the peninsula, topped by the ruins of three castles—former fortresses for Greeks, Franks and Venetians. Hotels now stand on the site. You can take a tunnel and then an elevator to admire the view from the top. Those who take the main road down pass an appealing Byzantine-Venetian **chapel,** sparkling like a gem in the sunset glow.

Epidauros *(Epídavros)*

Situated on a sleepy, pine-scented Argolid plain between two large hills about 30 kilometres from Náfplio, Epidauros is the legendary home of Asklepios (Aesculapius). This pastoral place does seem to exude a healthy aura, although the ancient town and spa have long since been reduced to ruins.

Epidauros' circular **theatre,** however, is one of the great marvels of Greece and one of its best-preserved monuments. Perfectly proportioned, it was constructed on a majestic scale by the architect Polykleitos the Younger in the 4th century B.C. It is still used in the high summer season for theatrical and musical performances during the celebrated Annual Festival of Greek Drama. Maria Callas and other world-renowned stars have performed in galas here, and week after

The Great Healer

Many centuries ago, Epidauros found fame as a place to which the ailing travelled from far and wide in the hopes of a miraculous cure. It all started with the mythological figure of Asklepios. Son of Apollo and a Boeotian princess named Koronis, Asklepios was nursed by goats and raised in Epidauros by the centaur Chiron, who taught him the powers of healing.

After the 6th century B.C., Asklepios developed into a cult figure for Greek healers, with Epidauros at the centre of the cult. Even today his caduceus or wand, entwined with serpents, is the official emblem for doctors of the Western world.

Afflicted people came to Epidauros for ritual purification, sacrifices to the gods and nights spent in a sacred dormitory, where they slept on the skins of sacrificial animals. Asklepios is said to have appeared to them in their dreams and revealed how they could be cured.

Snakes were supposedly used for curative invocations and perhaps even blood-letting. Treatment also included baths, physical exercise and games in a special arena, plus evening entertainment in the magnificent theatre.

week, visitors still thrill to the sight of the ancient Greek tragedies.

In the old days, important personages sat in the reddish stone thrones in the first row. A channel around the circular orchestra was used to drain off rainwater. The theatre, which can seat 14,000 spectators and is made up of 55 rows intersected by aisles to produce a "pie-wedge" effect, was built according to the golden rules of acoustics. Speaking or humming in a normal voice from the orchestra, you can still be heard perfectly by someone on the top row—74 feet (22½ m.) higher.

The pleasant, quiet **museum** displays a few relics from the site, as well as scale models of its antique temples, and inscriptions describing miraculous cures. You'll see parts of the circular *tholos,* a rotunda also by Polykleitos the Younger; the ruined foundations can be visited on the site outside. The *tholos'* erstwhile function is a mystery; some think curative rituals were performed there, possibly using snakes. Its mosaic pavement fragments shown in the museum are worth a look, as is the reconstruction of the inner ceiling, with Corinthian flowered decor.

On leaving the museum, you soon come to the ruins. The rocky remains are fairly sketchy, although with a map you can distinguish certain striking features of the former cure site. The first ruin, shaped like a large square, is the *katagogeion,* which probably served as a kind of hotel. Further on are ruins of Greek baths, the gymnasium and vestiges of a colonnaded court within which is a brick *odeion* built by the Romans.

Not much remains of the Temple of Asklepios, a Doric-style edifice, fragments of which are displayed in the museum. The roped off *tholos* is easy to spot; its rotunda was built in a series of concentric walls whose foundations are nearly intact.

Paleá Epídavros, the area's beach, where an ancient town lies buried under the sea, is a 10-kilometre drive to the northeast. It's a simple, modern village with a fisherman's bay and nearby campsite.

Mycenae *(Mikíne)*

Even on a blisteringly sunny day, the ruins of this once-regal ancient city are invested by a brooding sense of darkness and horror. Here Orestes commited the heinous crime of matricide, winding up a gory succession of family atrocities perpetrated by the members of the House of Atreus, the legendary rulers of

The theatre at Epidauros remains one of the marvels of Greece.

Mycenae. Some of the events described in Aeschlyos' famed *Oresteia* drama cycle are thought to be true. Mycenae is also described by Homer in the *Iliad* and *Odyssey*. It seems that Agamemnon really did exist as a king here and led troops in the Trojan War.

The Mycenaean civilization reached its zenith in the 2nd millennium B.C. The city's wealth is evident in the exquisite gold objects that are now a major attraction in Athens' National Archaeological Museum. The gold mask of Agamemnon is an unforgettable study in the chilling, fixed look of death.

Mycenae is only about 30 minutes or so by car from Náfplio. After the small modern town with several tavernas and hotels, you reach the foot of the **acropolis,** usually the first stop on any tour. You have to walk to the summit of the hill, 912 feet (278 m.) high and bordered by walls that are 26 feet (8 m.) wide in places. These enormous **walls,** made up of blocks weighing as much as 20 tons, are called "Cyclopean", because the Greeks believed that they could only have been built by the Cyclops, one-eyed giants of mythology.

Following French archaeological expeditions in 1828, the

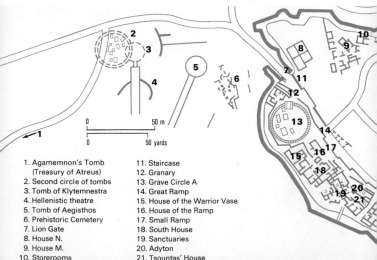

1. Agamemnon's Tomb (Treasury of Atreus)
2. Second circle of tombs
3. Tomb of Klytemnestra
4. Hellenistic theatre
5. Tomb of Aegisthos
6. Prehistoric Cemetery
7. Lion Gate
8. House N.
9. House M.
10. Storerooms
11. Staircase
12. Granary
13. Grave Circle A
14. Great Ramp
15. House of the Warrior Vase
16. House of the Ramp
17. Small Ramp
18. South House
19. Sanctuaries
20. Adyton
21. Tsountas' House

German Heinrich Schliemann —who also discovered Troy— started excavations at Mycenae in 1874. Two years later he had found evidence of the partially buried city; he brought to light tombs and skeletons and many objects of gold.

You enter the complex of palace ruins through the **Lion Gate,** a colossal monolithic limestone tympanum flanked by two standing headless lionesses of impressive dimensions. Through this gate you'll find the concentric stone circles that form the royal tombs of **Grave Circle A,** in which Schliemann found 19 skeletons. Archaeologists date these six

tombs to around the end of the 16th century B.C. The shaft graves also yielded furnishings, gold treasures and other burial objects. Below the gravesite, ruins of houses and a priests' dwelling have been found.

Proceeding upwards to the peak of the hill on the roughly cobbled royal road or great ramp, you reach the **main palace,** dating from the 15th century B.C. The great courtyard, open to the sky, leads into the *megaron* or inner royal chamber, where you can still see the bases of wooden columns which once supported a roof. With a bit of imagination, you can almost picture Klytem-

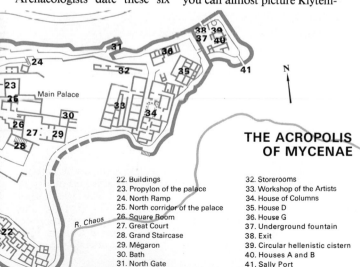

THE ACROPOLIS OF MYCENAE

22. Buildings
23. Propylon of the palace
24. North Ramp
25. North corridor of the palace
26. Square Room
27. Great Court
28. Grand Staircase
29. Mégaron
30. Bath
31. North Gate

32. Storerooms
33. Workshop of the Artists
34. House of Columns
35. House D
36. House G
37. Underground fountain
38. Exit
39. Circular hellenistic cistern
40. Houses A and B
41. Sally Port

nestra emerging from here, blood-stained from her husband's murder.

From here you can descend to the eastern fortress and cistern, whose 99 steps lead to a "secret" water source. The place is rather spooky, and most tourists don't make it down very far, even with a torch (flashlight).

Downhill from the Lion Gate are several **beehive tombs,** a striking feature of the site. "Klytemnestra's Tomb" is

so named for convenience. It's a 13th-century B.C. construction in the typically Mycenaean "beehive" shape—a circular, vaulted funerary chamber preceded by a long stone funnel entrance.

Heading back towards the village, you come to the **Treasury of Atreus,** also known as Agamemnon's Tomb, which has a separate paying entrance. This architectural masterpiece dated around 1300 B.C. is a highlight of the archaeological re-

The ruins of Mycenae have their terrible story to tell.

House of Horrors

The curse on the House of Atreus had its roots in the legend of Tantalos, son of Zeus, who served up his only son Pelops as a dish for the gods. Unappreciative of the gesture, the gods sent Tantalos to Hades to be tortured forever by hunger and thirst. Each time food or water came within reach, it would be whisked away before he could get a morsel to eat or a drop to drink. Furthermore Tantalos' descendants were doomed by a curse.

Pelops was restored to life, furnished with an ivory shoulder, since one of the goddesses, Demeter, had inadvertently eaten part of him during the loathsome feast. But the gods' fury fell with full force on Pelops' sons, Atreus and Thyestes. Thyestes seduced Atreus' wife; when Atreus found out he had been cuckolded by his brother, he killed Thyestes' young children and had them cut up and served to their father for dinner.

Atreus' progeny were Agamemnon, who led the Greeks in the Trojan War, and Menelaos, husband of Helen of Troy. Following his victory at Troy, Agamemnon returned to a hero's welcome in Mycenae. But he, too, had committed the horror of sacrificing his daughter Iphigenia in order to win the war. While he had been at war, his wife Klytemnestra had taken a lover, Aegisthos, and Agamemnon himself brought home a beautiful captive woman, Kassandra, daughter of Priam, King of Troy. Her predictions of doom for the House of Atreus—"The floor is red with blood," she shouted to elders and rabble at the palace gates—were to prove only too true. Klytemnestra killed Agamemnon to avenge the sacrifice of their daughter.

Klytemnestra and her lover reigned for several years, but her son Orestes, egged on by his sister Elektra, came back to kill his mother, in revenge for Agamemnon's death. He performed the deed with great misgivings and sorrow, and was long pursued by the Furies. Eventually he was accorded forgiveness by the goddess Athena. Thus ended the tragedy of the House of Atreus, the subject of Aeschylos' trilogy of plays, the *Oresteia,* which are still performed to this day, particularly at Epidauros.

mains in the Peloponnese and could conceivably have been Agamemnon's actual tomb.

You enter through the *dromos,* the typical Mycenaean long stone funnel leading deep into the hillside. The *tholos,* or circular interior, is reached through an impressive portal with a lintel of colossal monolithic stone blocks, one weighing nearly 120 tons. As you become accustomed to the cool darkness, you'll notice the awesome size and shape of the domed interior. Remarkably, the vault built in gradually diminishing circles of *breccia* stones—an amalgam of pebbles—was so perfect that no mortar was needed to join them. To the right of the entrance, guides point out the small chamber that could have been a burial place for a chief such as Agamemnon, or a treasury. It is thought that over the centuries the place was often looted, so that nobody can say what it contained.

The Mycenae area offers other ruins and tombs—for example, visitors can see sketchy remains of Grave Circle B, only discovered in 1951.

From Mycenae a small road leads off to Mt. Évia. Here stands the **Argive Heraion** *(Iréon),* the shrine to Hera, wife of Zeus and first among goddesses, a site much revered by the ancients. The upper of the two levels was once graced with a 5th-century B.C. temple and a huge gold and ivory statue of Hera. Although the site and the view are picturesque, little is left today, save the foundations and column bases of the temple; statues from here are displayed in Athens' National Archaeological Museum.

Tiryns *(Tírins)*

Rising proudly on the Argolid plain about 5 kilometres from Náfplio, this 60-foot (18-m.) plateau crowned by a citadel has been considered as the legendary birthplace and home of Herakles (Hercules), who is said to have rested here between his twelve labours.

The site was inhabited many millennia ago and refortified by the neighbouring Mycenaeans in the 13th and 12th centuries B.C. At that time the population reached about 15,000, but in 468 B.C., rival peoples from Argos invaded and destroyed Tiryns, blighting its importance forever.

You approach the "impregnable" ramparts along a wide stone ramp. After going through outer and inner gateways, you pass the eastern fortifications, which form a long

gallery made of enormous stone monoliths weighing 15 to 20 tons each, with six "pillbox" or vaulted chamber sections, probably once used for storage. The walls, 32 feet (10 m.) thick in places, are worthy of the term Cyclopean (see p. 44).

After a short walk past the fortifications, you'll reach ruins of the *propylon,* or monumental entrance, thought to be a model for the *propylaea* on the Acropolis in Athens. Two more courtyards lead into the *megaron,* the heart or inner chamber, which once had a central area for the king's throne. You can still see a trace of the circular royal altar.

Towards the main route are more **ramparts,** providing good views of the surrounding plain, and a secret passage staircase leading downhill.

Árgos

Built among rocky hills some 12 kilometres from Náfplio, Árgos does not attract many tourists, but those who discover the ruins near the modern town and the excellent museum are happy they stopped here.

According to legend, Argos was founded by Danaos, father of the Danaides—wilful women who murdered their husbands and were condemned in Hades to the perpetual labour of filling jugs with holes in them. These people supposedly originated in Egypt, and the ancients considered Argos to be Greece's oldest city. Rising to eminence around the 8th century B.C., Argos became ruler of the north-east Peloponnese and a formidable rival to Sparta.

On the outskirts of new Árgos, at the base of Lárisa hill you can see remains of 2nd-century A.D. **Roman baths,** equipped with sophisticated heating systems. The 4th-century B.C. **theatre** that graces the stony Lárisa slopes seated 20,000 spectators. At one point the Romans transformed the orchestra into a *naumachion* or pool for aquatic contests and displays. The site is also marked by traces of an *odeion* from the 3rd or 2nd century B.C.

Lárisa Kástro dominates the scene from a height of 905 feet (276 m.), topped by a medieval citadel. Built by Franks in the 13th and 14th centuries on the site of an ancient acropolis, it is still studded with remains from subsequent Venetian and Turkish fortifications. From the summit, on a clear day, you can admire a panoramic view of the Argolid plains and the bay of Náfplio.

In Árgos, the **museum** in **49**

Odós Ólgas is a recent gift from the French School of Archaeology. The ground floor exhibits finds from ancient Argos, especially objects from the Protogeometric and Geometric periods, including many amphorae and vases. Look out for the extraordinary 13th-century B.C. *kourotrophos,* a small, simple and elegant statue of a nursing mother. A large fragment of a clay *krater,* a wide-mouthed vessel, is adorned with a Cyclops whose one eye is being cheerfully gouged out by Odysseus. In the museum garden you'll see attractive Roman mosaics depicting Bacchus, the four seasons and hunting scenes.

The Arcadian Coast

From ÁSTROS (about 30 km. from Náfplio), a well-paved road leads down a coastal area of extraordinary beauty, still unspoiled by tourism. Go on a clear day, and for about two hours before reaching Leonídio, you'll be treated to spectacular views.

Mt. Párnon towering above much of the coast culminates at 6,350 feet (1,935 m.); it's said that wolves still roam on its forested upper slopes. Several fishing villages such as TÍROU and SAMBATIKÍ offer picturesque sites, bathing areas and

tavernas. **Leonídio** (3,200 inhabitants) is beautifully situated between a river and a ruddy, rocky mountainside. It's a little gem of a town, with a restored 12th-century fortress, quaint houses with balconies and red-tile roofs, and old-fashioned shops and cafés.

Nearby Saronic Islands

Póros, Spétse and Hydra are all within reach of Náfplio. You can easily visit Póros on a day trip. The best way to combine Spétse and Hydra is to drive to PORTOCHÉLI (about 1½ hours), leave your car—which is not allowed on either island —and take the hydrofoil first to Spétse, where you should spend at least a night to enjoy the sights. The following day you go on to Hydra (again, you might want to stay longer than a few hours), returning to Portochéli to pick up your car and continue your journey in the Peloponnese.

Póros

The road from Náfplio leads you on a two-hour drive of considerable beauty, especially after you emerge from the dry, rocky landscape to glimpse the sea gleaming below. A five-minute ferry crossing from GALATÁS village brings you to **Póros** port, a teeming and lively place of whitewashed or pastel houses piled up on the pine-covered hills.

Bays and coves on this tiny island are exquisite. A long hike or short drive will take you to the remains of the **Temple of Poseidon,** where the orator Demosthenes, who championed Athenian independence from Macedonia, committed suicide in 322 B.C.

Near Póros town is the **Monastery of the Virgin,** blinding-white in its green hilltop setting above the sea, surrounded by huge cypresses and pines. It is still inhabited by a few monks who tolerate tourists as long as they're discreet in dress and behaviour.

Spétse

Refreshingly green, Spétse was known by the ancient Greeks as "Pine-Covered Island". The island offers no archaeological sites, so it attracts more holidaying Athenian families than tourists, but it's an ideal spot for relaxing in the sun, cycling, boating or just enjoying the scenery.

Spétse is known for its important role in the 1821 uprising, being the first of the local islands to revolt against the Turks. Two of **Spétse's** elegant old mansions (some of which once belonged to ship-owners) are still the property of descendants of Bouboulina, the courageous lady admiral whose fleet vanquished the Turks in 1822.

Transport is by horse-drawn carriage or donkey, but recent permission for motorcycles has detracted somewhat from the former quiet charm. Clip-clopping in a horse-carriage or walking around the small but lively centre of town, you'll notice some decorative mosaic sidewalks, plenty of boutiques, cafés and tavernas.

The whole island can be enjoyed for its lovely scenery—with aleppo pines, cypresses and oleanders in ample supply. Don't miss a walk or ride by rented bicycle to the very picturesque **old port,** east of the town centre. Besides brightly painted houses, you'll see some appealing churches in the white Greek Orthodox island style.

West of the centre of town is an exclusive boys' school founded by two local millionaires. The English novelist John Fowles taught here in the early '60s and was inspired to write his novel *The Magus.* You can also see where the fictional Magus, a kind of latter-day magician, might have lived —in a villa on the other side of the island near two lovely beaches—**Ágii Angíri** and 51

Agía Paraskeví, both reached by daily motor launch or bus. The launch passes by Spetsopoúla, a private island belonging to the shipping magnate Stavros Niarchos.

Hydra *(Ídra)*

This 18-kilometre-long island is essentially a big rock, but has enough attractions to make it a favourite with both Greek and foreign holiday-makers.

The main town is also called **Hydra.** The spectacular bay in a deep, rocky trough topped by windmills and churches has been compared to the French port of St. Tropez. With a reputation as an artists' colony, it does indeed have a theatrical, "arty-crafty" air, and it also proposes some attractive boutiques and at least two or three outstanding restaurants, the best anywhere in or around the Peloponnese.

Hydra outlaws motor vehicles, and all transport is effected by donkeys, mules or people. A human porter or donkey will help you and your luggage to your hotel. The Venetian houses with their brightly painted doorstoops and balconies lining sinuous

There's always plenty going on
52 *in Hydra's port.*

streets make an enchanting sight against the mountain backdrop.

Sere and barren, Hydra is not idyllic for casual walkers or bathers, and the rocky swimming ledges near the main harbour tend to be crowded in summer. But you can escape by taking a hired boat to one of the deserted coves around the island where the water is clear, the underwater scenery a delight and the surroundings starkly beautiful.

Splash of colour in Hydra. Taking the scenic route to Kalávrita.

The North Coast

Several seaside resorts dot the north coast of the Peloponnese, which runs from Corinth to Pátra, but they are not very appealing. However, a detour up the Vouraikós Valley to Kalávrita is well worth the trip.

Kalávrita

The small town of Kalávrita (2,000 inhabitants) is happily situated in a breeze-cooled spot on the Vouraikós River, 2,460 feet (750 m.) up in the Aroánia range. To reach Kalávrita, you might drive up a **scenic route** from TRÁPEZA, but those who want to enjoy the awesome

scenery and some heart-stopping thrills besides should take the **narrow-gauge railway** from the town of Diakoftó. The railway, built in the late 19th century, is an astonishing engineering accomplishment, which you'll appreciate as the train labours for about 13 kilometres up wildly beautiful gorges, through tunnels and past striated escarpments. The train stops at Méga Spíleo and then at Kalávrita (about 1½ hours in all). It is best to visit Kalávrita and environs first and then descend to Méga Spíleo.

Kalávrita is remembered for a tragic massacre on December 13, 1943, when occupying German troops killed 1,436 males over the age of 15 and burned down the town. The hands of the main church clock have been halted at 2.34, the hour of the atrocity. Since rebuilt, the town is now a cheery place, with a central square full of greenery and cafés.

From here you can hire a taxi for the ride to **Agía Lávra,** the monastery celebrated as the site where Germanos, Archbishop of Pátra, is said to have raised the standard of revolt against the Turks on March 25, 1821. The archbishop's action was taken as a signal for national rebellion, thus sparking off the War of Independence. (The

monastery can also be reached by donkey or foot from the little railway station—a tough uphill hike of 45 minutes.)

Forbidding though it looks, Méga Spíleo offers a cordial welcome.

Today's monastery is a restoration of the original 10th-century Byzantine building, burned down in both 1826 and 1943. An ancient plane tree fills up a good deal of the entry court. The **museum** inside contains some elaborate icons, and near the crypt outside you'll see some macabre but well-preserved skeletons of monks.

The taxi can then take you down to **Méga Spíleo.** Perched on a sheer escarpment, this monastery is dramatically situated if somewhat starkly modern in aspect. A miraculous icon was found here in a cave in the 4th century, hence the name, which means "Great Cavern". Under the Paleologues (see p. 22), the monastery reached its apogee; it seems that the despots liked to retreat here for rest and meditation. The monastery was destroyed by fire in 1934, but has been rebuilt.

The few monks in residence will provide you with something to cover up with if you look skimpily clad, and will cheerfully show you around. The **museum** displays some striking icons, Byzantine illuminations and elaborate vestments. Beautifully cool and lovingly tended by the monks, the **grotto** below the main monastery contains a fountain and religious statues.

You can walk or hire a donkey for the rocky descent back to the tiny railway station, for a return train journey to the coast. Or you can opt for a bus or taxi back to Trápeza.

Pátra

The largest city of the Peloponnese, with a population of 141,000, Pátra is the main Greek port on the Ionian Sea. In history it played an important role in the Achaean League, and in 1205 it became a Frankish barony. It was sold to the Venetians in 1408, later coming under the rule of the Paleologos brothers (1429). The Turks took over in 1460.

Today the bustling city has little to offer the visitor save many shops and a few hotels, though the squares are not unattractive.

To the west of the seaport in a green square is a large, neo-Byzantine church (1979), **Ágios Andréas**—the pride of Pátra. St. Andrew the Apostle spent his last years in the area and died as a martyr in Pátra.

A few blocks above the seaport you can find the site of an ancient acropolis topped by a 9th-century Byzantine **fortress** *(kástro)*, encompassing two churches. The fortress was enlarged by Franks, Venetians and Turks; you can see the differing styles in what remains today. The lower tower and bastion afford good views over Pátra all the way to the island of Zákinthos.

Some 7 kilometres to the north-east of Pátra lies **Río**, terminus for ferries to Antírio. It's also a holiday resort with some fair beaches and the Kástro Moréas, a 15th-century Turkish castle surrounded by a moat.

Killíni Peninsula

KILLÍNI lies about 65 kilometres from Pátra. The peninsula on which it stands, the westernmost point of the Peloponnese, is a beautiful place to visit, with green slopes clad in olive and fruit trees sweeping down to long stretches of beach.

The whole area was of considerable importance in the Middle Ages. From the 13th to 15th centuries, Killíni (then called Clarence) served as the main port of the Peloponnese under the Villehardouins, the Angevins of Naples and finally **57** the Venetians. It was an essential stop on the maritime route to the Orient and hosted a mixture of sailors, merchants, artists, knights and beggars. Today the heart of ancient Clarence itself is little more than rubble, to which it was partially reduced by Constantine Paleologos (one of the Despots of Mistra) in 1430.

The little modern village of KÁSTRO is dominated by the old fortress of **Chlemoútsi** (also called Clermont), a well-preserved typical Frankish construction dominating the top of the Chelonátas hill. The castle was built between 1220 and 1223 by Geoffroi II de Villehardouin; in the late 13th century it went to the Angevins of Naples. In 1427 it fell into the hands of Constantine Paleologos, but was taken in 1460 by the Turks, who reconstructed some walls to make room for artillery. The Venetians gave the fortress the name Castel Tornese. Destroyed again in 1825 by Ibrahim Pasha, the fort is now being gradually restored. Seen from afar, the deserted bastions seem rather eerie, with cawing crows wheeling around the old stones.

You enter the fortress through a huge vaulted gateway. On the left are the remains of a two-storey chapel; the servants sat below, the masters upstairs. The long gallery on the right served as guardroom below, with the main reception rooms upstairs.

The hexagonal courtyard was once the scene of revels, juggling and other entertainments put on for the despots. All around the courtyard are huge barrel-vaulted galleries—also once two-storey, but with no dividing floor left. To one side a dungeon is being excavated.

A stairway from the grassy courtyard leads to the **terraces** from where you can enjoy splendid vistas of the Elidian plains, broken by citrus and cypress groves. Sometimes you can see the island of Zákinthos in the distance.

VARTHOLOMIÓ, a rather picturesque village nearby, has a colourful weekly market, a Greek Orthodox church and a typical *platía* or village square. LOUTRÁ KILLÍNIS has a group of Roman baths built on mineral springs in a verdant pine setting.

Kyllíni Golden Beach Hotel is more resort than modern hotel and gives access to a fabulous stretch of truly golden sandy **beach,** where you don't

Tourists and locals find their own forms of relaxation.

have to stray far from the sun-bathers to see shepherds and their flocks in the greenery just above. The resort makes a good base for excursions around the Peloponnese.

Zákinthos

You can reach Zákinthos (also known as Zante) by ferry from Killíni (1½ hours). A delightful island of plains, mountains and excellent beaches, Zákinthos is called "Flower of the Levant". The Venetians, who occupied the island from 1489 to 1797, endowed it with a legacy of highly cultivated artistic activity. In the 18th and 19th centuries it was a centre for Italian and Greek poets.

ZÁKINTHOS, the capital and main port, is an attractive reconstruction of the old Venetian city, largely destroyed by an earthquake in 1953. The ancient Venetian fortress, the **Kástro,** provides wonderful views of the city, the bay and coast all the way down to Pílos. The **Museum of Byzantine Art** contains relics of the old town, a rich collection of icons and some old frescoes from various local churches. **Kiría ton Angélon** (Church of Our Lady of the Angels) is known for its elegant Renaissance façade and rich iconostasis dating from the 17th century.

Olympia *(Olimpía)*

Lying in a lush, green valley, where the Alpheios *(Alfiós)* and Kladéos rivers meet, Olympia is one of Greece's glories, blessed by both nature and man, and a truly appropriate choice of the ancients for the worship of their greatest god and goddess, Zeus and Hera.

You'll find modern OLIMPÍA, a little town of considerable charm, nestling under Mt. Krónos. But all roads lead to Ancient Olympia, best seen at sunset when the temple stones and other ruins are tinged with a soft golden glow.

Ancient Olympia

Immediately after the entrance to the excavations, you'll see the remains of Roman baths. A path indicates where there was once a covered running track which formed the east wing of the Gymnasium, a quadrangle with some column capitals still around. From here head for the **Palaestra,** or wrestling school, marked by a 19-column Doric colonnade. Passing the ruin of a priests' house, you reach Phidias' Workshop, where the Golden Age sculptor is said to have worked on the gigantic statue of Zeus that once stood in the temple here. The studio was later turned into a Byzantine church, identifiable by some elaborate Byzantine masonry.

The Leonidaion, built by Leonidas of Naxos in the 4th century B.C., may have been a vast hostelry for visitors. You can see where the rooms were once grouped around an atrium with a circular pond. Take a look at the Bouleuterion, a meeting-place for judges and administrators of the games.

The Sanctuary, or Altis, is the high point of any visit. The 5th-century B.C. **Temple of Zeus** has not one column standing, yet it's still a stunning sight, with the drums and capitals of Doric columns tumbled

down like a house of cards—the result of the earthquake in the 6th century. The temple's dimensions—210 feet (64 m.) long by 92 feet (28 m.) wide—nearly equal those of the Parthenon. It featured a peristyle or colonnaded exterior of 13 fluted shell-limestone columns at either side, six at each end. The pediment statuary found during archaeological digs now make outstanding exhibits in the nearby museum.

The temple's three-naved *cella* or sanctuary once contained such a monumental statue of Zeus sculpted by Phidias that it was considered one of the Seven Wonders of

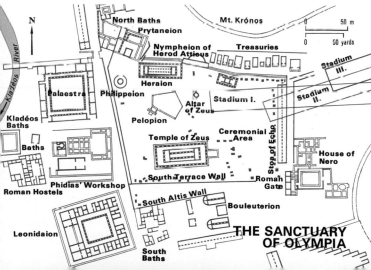

THE SANCTUARY OF OLYMPIA

the Ancient World. Only a privileged few were allowed to view the colossus. Zeus draped in ivory and gold was seated on an ebony and ivory throne holding a sceptre topped by an eagle in one hand and a winged victory in the other. Nothing remains of this awesome work except some bas-reliefs from the throne now in the Hermitage in Leningrad.

Towards the mountain, you can see what's left of the circular Philippeion, a small votive monument in Ionic style, dating from the 4th century B.C.

The **Heraion** or Temple of Hera is one of the best-preserved buildings on the site. It was built in typical Archaic style around 600 B.C. at the foot of Mt. Krónos; several of the massive fluted columns have been restored to standing position. The temple, 164 feet (50 m.) long, contained many effigies of the goddess and Zeus, plus a famed statue of Hermes by Praxiteles. You can see some of these works at the local museum.

Continue to the **Nympheion of Herod Atticus** built by a rich Athenian in A.D. 160; once encircled by colonnades and statues, it consists of a semi-circular fountain surrounded by ponds where water was col-

lected from the springs on Mt. Krónos. Further along stand ruins of 12 Doric-columned **treasuries,** which were erected by various Greek cities and colonies as votive offerings to the gods. Below the raised terrace of the treasuries are the bases of statues to Zeus, financed by fines collected for cheating.

The **Stadium** was the world's first as we know it, and joggers still enjoy doing laps round its circuit. The main entrance is a restoration of a vaulted passageway, originally built in the 4th century B.C.; the lone arch you see today dates from Roman times—only athletes and judges were allowed to enter here. The Stadium could accommodate up to 40,000 spectators who sat on the sloped embankments; on the right of the entry were marble seats reserved for the judges. South of the Stadium are a few traces of the Hippodrome, where horse and chariot races were staged.

The **museum,** opened in 1972 across the main road from the ruins and not far from the older museum higher up on the hill, is a well-planned spacious home for the stunning sculptures it holds.

The star attraction has to be the 5th-century B.C. pediment sculpture in Parian marble from the Temple of Zeus. The **west pediment** features the Centauromachy, the mythological drunken brawl in which the Centaurs (half-man, half-horse) were invited to a wedding by the Lapiths, got drunk and tried to abduct the bride and other female guests. Apollo stands bolt upright in the centre, disdainfully extending an imperious arm. Examine the whole thing in detail: the mass of figures seethes with a sense of powerful but contained violence—so perfect and

Vestiges of former glory can be seen in Olympia's Heraion.

The Games

Legend has it that after the indomitable Herakles had cleaned up the Augean stables (which had been allowed by their owner, Elis, to accumulate 30 years of filth), he built a sacred shrine in the Altis ("Holy Grove") for the cults honouring Zeus, Hera and Pelops. Olympia grew up around this shrine and gained fame for the sporting contests held in its precincts.

It is thought that athletic events began at the Olympic site in the Mycenaean era, but the official Olympic Games were not inaugurated until 776 B.C. From then on, every four years, the peoples of Greece ceased hostilities, while spectators as well as athletes came to Olympia from all over the ancient world.

Contestants often surrounded themselves with elaborate entourages. Winners were adulated with the same enthusiasm shown for today's top athletes: they received valuable prizes along with a crown of wild olive and had statues built in their honour. Women were excluded.

The race track measured 600 Olympic feet (192.27 m.). Sports other than running included boxing and horse and chariot racing. The pentathlon featured long jump, javelin-throwing, sprinting, discus-throwing and wrestling. The contests reached their zenith in the 5th century B.C.

Later, attendant events were added such as painting exhibitions and poetry competitions, but by this time corruption and decadence were setting in and the original religious aspect of the games was losing its significance.

The Byzantine Emperor Theodosius ended the games by edict in 393 A.D. In the 6th century an earthquake toppled the remains of the great Temple of Zeus, and subsequent flooding left silt deposits covering the whole site. It wasn't until the early 19th century that excavations by French, and later German, teams got under way.

In 1896—with the encouragement of the French Baron Pierre de Coubertin and Greek approval—the quadrennial games were revived in Athens; they have since taken place (at different venues around the world) every four years, except for brief interruptions during the two world wars.

Following political wrangling over the modern games, some have suggested that they should return permanently to their original site at Olympia.

yet so alive that people viewing it have been moved to tears.

The **east pediment** opposite is a less fraught but also excellent rendering of the chariot race between Pelops and Oinomaos. The characters look poised in a moment of time before Hippodamia's fate is decided.

Visitors also flock to see Praxiteles' **Hermes** (dated about 340 B.C.), the graceful marble statue found in the Temple of Hera. Hermes, Zeus' wing-footed messenger, stands holding the child Dionysus, with his garment draped over a cut-off tree trunk, his relaxed body filled with a balanced grace.

Other high points in the museum include the fluidly carved winged **Nike** ("Victory") by Paionios (around 420 B.C.), and the lively statue of **Zeus and Ganymede** (470 B.C.) in fine-grained fired clay, depicting a determined god abducting his favourite small boy to Olympos to become a cupbearer. You can't miss the colossal 6th-century B.C. **Head of Hera.**

The **bronze rooms** are another extraordinary feature of the museum, with many 5th-century B.C. statuettes full of expression and grace. You'll see a handsome horse votive offering (470-460 B.C.), a young runner at the starting line, older bronze bas-relief plaques of a charioteer (7th century B.C.), and fine decorated breastplates, helmets and masks.

Bassae *(Vassé)*

An excursion for the adventurous and temple-lovers, Bassae can be reached in less than two hours from Olympia.

Head south-east to ANDRÍTSENA. Fourteen kilometres further on, you come to Bassae itself, a Classical temple ruin in a desolate, rocky site, 3,710 feet (1,132 m.) up on Mt. Kotílion. Built in the mid-5th century B.C., it is said to have been designed by Iktinos, the architect of the Parthenon in Athens. It was supposedly commissioned by citizens of nearby Phigaleia in gratitude to Apollo for saving them from the plague. Forgotten for centuries on its isolated site, the temple was not rediscovered until 1765. Much of the sculpture is now in the British Museum.

The Doric-style **temple** in grey limestone is exceptionally narrow; the columns number 15 on each side to only six at each end. Another exception: it's orientation is north-south; most temples are east-west. In 1975 restoration began on the edifice, which was in imminent danger of collapse. **65**

The West Coast

An asphalt road leads down the west coast of the Peloponnese from Pírgos to Kiparissía on the way south from Olympia. Those who want to get away from the crowds like this route because along most of the coast stretches a near-deserted sandy beach. A few small settlements, tavernas and beach houses are the only evidence of civilization you'll see for miles.

Just off the road, about 30 kilometres south of Pírgos, you might stop off at the spa town of LOUTRÁ KAIÁFAS. Through a pine forest you'll spot a couple of lagoons and lakes bordered by oleanders, pines and a few simple hotels. People apparently come here more for the rest than for the cure.

From here the scenery gets

The "beehive" tomb is a typical construction of the Mycenaean era.

progressively more beautiful, with slopes covered in olive trees, cypresses and scrub oaks down to the sea. Just above KIPARISSÍA hangs an old Frankish-Byzantine **fort** alongside the remains of a small Greco-Roman theatre. A picturesque, narrow road takes you up to the fort to admire Kiparissía from above, a town of red-roofed houses edged by the deep blue sea on one side, sloping green hills dotted with cypresses on the other.

After the town of GARGA-LIÁNI, take a signposted road to CHÓRA to see the **museum,** perched on a quiet hilltop. It contains some fine jewellery and gold objects from the Mycenaean era found at Nestor's Palace and other nearby archaeological sites.

Nestor's Palace

Nestor's Palace on the plateau of Englianós is disappointingly mundane today. For preservation reasons, the **ruins** are covered with a corrugated iron roof.

The site was discovered in 1939 by an American team, and excavations began in 1952. Dating from early Mycenaean times, the palace burned down around 1200 B.C., although stone column bases and parts of the original floor survive.

The palace's most illustrious inhabitant—after whom the edifice is named—was wise old King Nestor, who commanded the second largest of the fleets that sailed against Troy, despite his great age.

Like those at Tiryns and Mycenae, the palace comprised courtyards, storage and living areas and a royal sector with a throne area or *megaron,* in which you'll see a round clay hearth, once surrounded by four columns. Also notice traces of a stone bath, possibly used by the queen.

According to archaeological finds, the decor in this palace and its apartments was elaborate and colourful, featuring bright frescoes of athletes, warriors and musicians. Unfortunately, nothing of this remains.

Pílos

Also known as Navaríno or Neókastro, Pílos is a charming seaport town of 2,300 inhabitants. It was built by the French in 1829 on a rise near the end of a promontory guarded by a ruined castle.

The strategic importance of Pílos' 6-kilometre-long bay was recognized in the Middle Ages. At that time the town stood on the north promontory, on a site known as Paleókastro. From the 16th to 18th centuries, the **67** area was disputed by the Venetians and the Turks—who in 1573 had built a fortress called Neókastro on the south promontory. On October 20, 1827, the allied forces of England, France and Russia routed the Egyptian-Turkish naval forces based here. The allies won the Battle of Navaríno by an astonishing margin: 6,000 Turks died to only 174 of the allies.

Tempting displays at a streetside stall. Opposite: Lantern dome tops tile-roofed church at Pílos.

The **main square** of present-day Pílos, called "Three Admirals" in honour of the victors of the battle in 1827, is a shady place to sit at a café sipping *oúzo* and watching the ships and yachts come in.

Spare the time for a walk up to **Neókastro,** restored by the French and used until recently as a prison. From the outer bastion you have a magnificent view over the bay and surroundings.

In season, little boats take visitors over to Paleókastro and the island of Sfaktiría. **Paleókastro** is on a rocky promontory connected to the mainland but accessible only by

boat. Here stood the ancient castle and settlement. From the 6th to 9th centuries A.D. the town harboured a Slav-Avar colony; a Frankish castle was constructed towards 1278. The town was held mainly by Venetians until 1715 when the Turks took over.

It's a 30-minute walk up to the former castle, also called Port de Junch, boasting ruined crenellated walls and square towers. A walk further north brings you to the **Grotto of Nestor,** a cave bristling with stalactites and stalagmites, whose animal-like shapes inspired the legend that the old sage, King Nestor, sheltered his cows here.

Sfaktiría (also called Sfagía) offers little of interest save several commemorative monuments to Greek and French soldiers from the Navaríno battle. At the summit of the hill lie the vestiges of an ancient fortress. From the boat, look down into the waters of the bay for glimpses of ships wrecked during the battle.

Methóni

Methóni is just a 20-minute drive south of Pílos. The modern town is pleasant but unexciting, although its adjacent arc of golden, sandy beach, with a couple of simple hotel-restaurants looking out over a group of small green islands, offers one of the prettiest seaside vistas in the Peloponnese.

In legend, old Methone (called Pedasos by Homer) was one of the seven cities promised by Agamemnon to his rival Achilles, as appeasement during the Trojan War. It was razed by the Venetians in 1125, before which it had served as a refuge for pirates. Frankish leader Geoffroi de Villehardouin made Methóni a bishopric and used the town as a base, although officially the Venetians held sway. They fortified the stronghold, known as Modon, and kept it as their own until the Turkish army captured it in 1500 after a month-long bombardment. Methóni alternated between Turkish and Venetian rule, until in 1828 it was finally taken from the Turkish general Ibrahim Pasha by the French, who partially rebuilt the town and fort.

You can't miss the dramatic approach to the **fortress** or citadel on its picturesque promontory. A big stone bridge with arches built by the French over a 15th-century moat leads up to the monumental Venetian gateway.

The rampart ahead is contained within two large bastions for storing artillery. High fortress walls guard the way through two more monumental gates to the main open esplanade, the site of the medieval town. To the right of the entry you'll see the fortified castle wall; ahead, the striking monolithic granite pillar once served as a stand for the Venetian lion of St. Mark.

By the sea are remains of a Turkish bath, cisterns and a ruined church. Scattered around the vast and rather desolate-looking grounds are several stone beehive-shaped structures, covering cisterns and perhaps once used as arms caches.

Looming at the southernmost end of the enceinte over a wooden bridge is the **Boúrdzi Tower,** a handsome hexagonal fortification reconstructed by the Turks in the 16th century. However, it's mainly a backdrop for scenic photography, since there is nothing inside the tower and it is prohibited to climb up for a view.

For further explorations on the Messinian peninsula, you can go over to **Koróni**—an old fortified village on a promontory, with much the same history as Methóni's.

Cars rarely disturb the sunlit peace of Koróni village.

The South

Few organized tours include the three southern prongs of the Peloponnese on itineraries; some do go to Sparta and Mistra, and the occasional cruise ship puts in at Gíthio. But independent travellers seeking tranquillity and dramatic landscapes are well advised to set aside a few days to visit the area.

The three promontories represent three distinct regions, and the inhabitants retain fiercely independent ways. Each region offers attractions of its own.

Capital of Messinía, **Kalamáta** (population 42,000) sits in the crook of the Gulf of Messinía. The modern city was once an important Frankish base and ducal court; Guillaume de Villehardouin (1218–1287) was born and died here. The town is nowadays famous for its olives.

On an isolated spur above the plain, the ancient Frankish château or *kástro* consists of a few remaining walls built by the Venetians and part of the original Frankish dungeon. If you have an hour or so to spend in town, you might visit the colourful market in the centre; the nearby museum housed in an old mansion displays antique and archaeological objects.

Messene

Few tourists make it to the out-of-the-way ruined city at Messene (not to be confused with modern Messíni, 25 km. to the south). After deserted roads and lunar landscapes of rock outcrops, MAVROMMÁTI is a welcome oasis with its sprinkling of houses and a lone café. A signposted footpath leads you down to the ancient site under Mt. Ithómi.

The city of Messene was traditionally an enemy of Sparta. Epaminondas—who led an army to victory over the Spartans in 371 B.C.—had the area built up as one of several strongholds, along with Megalopolis and Argos, to contain Sparta's power. Like the celebrated Epidauros, this ancient complex was dedicated to Asklepios and his curative powers.

Today the ruins are deserted, but the setting is still wonderful. The extensive **walls,** more than 9 kilometres in length, enclose the remains of the former fortress-city. At the end of the dirt road lies the **Sanctuary of Asklepios,** quiet nowadays save for a few donkeys and buzzing bees. In this pastoral setting, you can see the vestiges of a semicircular temple and an *odeion,* used for various rites in Hellenistic times.

Take a look at the little graveyard by the path as you go out; every grave is an original monument, decorated with pictures of the deceased and glass boxes displaying their favourite objects, including *oúzo* and coke bottles.

Hikers or those seeking a good view can climb nearly 2,630 feet (800 m.) up a rough path to the top of **Mt. Ithómi** to admire the scenery and to see the old Vourkáno Monastery, now abandoned.

Sparta *(Spárti)*

The Langáda Gorge road from Kalamáta to Sparta takes about one and a half hours. The views can be thrilling: rocky ravines rising steeply above the tumultuous Langáda River, chapels gleaming white on hillsides, and high, cool pine forests.

Today's Sparta has little in common with its bellicose ancestor, although there is a big army base on the plain nearby. Situated under the Taígetos peaks on a broad plain in Lakonía, it's a modern city of 13,000 inhabitants, with broad, clean streets and a central square edged by the colourful red and white town hall and several cafés. Head for the square during the evening stroll for some relaxed people-watching.

Barely two blocks away the

Belligerent Spartans

The very word Spartan immediately conjures up the image of the fiercely brave and frugal people of the ancient world, who disciplined themselves into a collective human war machine, terrorizing their neighbours for three centuries. The population was divided into three classes: the *Spartiatai*, who governed and owned land, the *perioikoi,* the shopkeepers and artisans, and Helots, who worked the lands belonging to the *Spartiatai*, leaving them the time to devote to physical and military training.

Boys were raised in military camps from the age of seven —and those unfit for service were left to die on the mountains. On reaching the terrible rites of adolescence, they were flogged—sometimes to death—and left to wander about on the hillsides alone, proving their manhood by living by their wits, until they either died or were welcomed back as soldiers. They were not considered soldier-citizens until the age of 30.

Many sources contend that Sparta's downfall around the 4th century B.C. was caused mainly by the ever-looser morals of the women, who loved luxury and refused to adhere to Spartan disciplinary traditions.

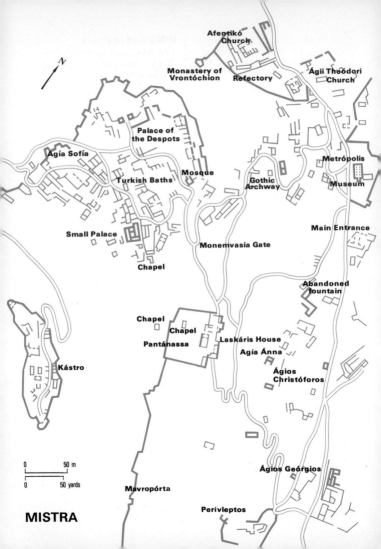

N

Afentikó
Church

Monastery of
Vrontóchion   Refectory

Ágii Theódori
Church

Palace of
the Despots

Ágia Sofía

Metrópolis

Mosque

Turkish Baths

Gothic
Archway

Museum

Small Palace

Main Entrance

Monemvasía Gate

Chapel

Abandoned
fountain

Chapel

Kástro

Chapel

Pantánassa

Laskáris House

Agía Ánna

Ágios
Christóforos

Ágios Geórgios

0   50 m

0   50 yards

Mavropórta

Perívleptos

MISTRA

Archaeological Museum—in a peaceful, quiet garden setting—contains local finds, such as Archaic bas-reliefs from the 6th century B.C., notably one of Helen of Troy and Menelaos, plus a good head of Apollo or Dionysos (4th century B.C.), discovered in 1978.

To the north of town lie some **ruins:** the "Tomb of Leonidas" is actually just the remains of a Hellenistic temple; a modern statue to Leonidas —the heroic Spartan king— stands not far away. About a kilometre futher north, vestiges of an **acropolis** marked "Ancient Sparta" are hidden away in an olive grove. The small site offers a ruined 1st-century A.D. temple, a 2nd-century B.C. theatre, the foundations of a temple to Athena and remains of a 10th-century Byzantine monastery standing among pine and eucalyptus trees.

Mistra *(Mistrás)*

This splendid medieval Byzantine city perched on a steep hill has been partially restored, and multi-domed ruddy brick churches topped by scalloped tile roofs contrast strikingly with green grassy slopes.

The fortress at Mistra was begun in A.D. 1249 by the Frankish leader Guillaume de Villehardouin, who aimed to control Lakonía from an impregnable fortress above the Evrótas valley. After Guillaume was captured in 1259 by Michael Paleologos, Byzantine forces held sway for several centuries. In the 14th and 15th centuries, the Paleologue despots ruled most of the empire from here. They made Mistra into a cultural haven, building churches in the shape of the Orthodox cross, with several domes and elaborate and lively interior decoration—an innovation from past Byzantine static formalism.

In 1460 Dimitri Paleologos ceded Mistra to the Turks. The churches were turned into mosques; pashas moved into the despots' palace. Despite some setbacks, a flourishing silk industry kept the city prosperous and populous (with 40,000 inhabitants) well into the 17th century. The Venetians occupied Mistra briefly from 1687 to 1715.

During the Russo-Turkish war, the Russians incited the Mainotes to rise and take Mistra in 1769. The Turks called in an Albanian army, who put down the rebellion and set Mistra on fire. The city was sacked by Ibrahim Pasha in 1825, and the remaining few citizens moved out when new Sparta was founded in 1834.

Mistra's Byzantine monuments dominate the plains of Sparta.

You might visit the lower town of old Mistra first, then drive to the top to see Agía Sofía and the upper town and fort. To see everything takes more or less a full day.

Lower Mistra

If you decide to start in the lower town, the classic first stop would be the **Metrópolis** or Cathedral of Ágios Dimítrios. In the flowered courtyard take a look at the fountain—installed in the 19th century even though the town was soon to be abandoned—and the ancient

and KARDAMÍLI, a tiny fishing village lined with old houses and a few churches above a rushing river. The 18th-century Ágios Spíridon church is remarkable for its slim bell-tower and exterior bas-reliefs, and further along Ágios Dimítrios is a 13th-century gem set in greenery overlooking the Gulf of Messinía opposite Koróni. And then on to Areópoli and the Máni itself.

To the Greeks this prong of the Peloponnese is more like a thorn, with its tradition of stub-

Pantánassa nuns live a frugal life devoted to prayer and embroidery.

born independence and rebelliousness among the inhabitants. For centuries they kept to forbidding eyries in the wild, rocky landscape, occasionally venturing forth to do battle when their interests were at stake. Today most mountain dwellings are deserted.

Composed mainly of barren rock rising to heights of 4,000 feet (1,214 m.), the Máni is a projection of the Taígetos range. The region is dotted with the ruins of at least 800 medieval and 17th-century watchtowers, around which people formed village governments under a chieftain. Disputes and blood vendettas were a way of life, so it's not surprising that many of the men were corsairs and adventurers who emigrated in the 18th century to Corsica—similar to the Máni in its rocky landscape and harsh customs.

These tough-living Maniotes were latter-day descendants of the Spartans, hounded from Lakonía in the 7th century A.D. by invading Slavs. Since then they gave no ground, either to the Franks (who nevertheless put up castles in the region) or to the Byzantines or Venetians. In the 18th century the Turks were able to conquer all of Greece except for the Máni. Enthusiastic participants in the 1821 uprising and War of Independence, the Maniotes nevertheless were reluctant to join the Greek kingdom formed after independence, and were convinced only by arm-twisting "negotiations".

Gíthio

Most tourists make this lively little seaside town (pronounced YEE-thio) the base for seeing the Máni. In Spartan times it was a major trade centre and naval base, especially during the Peloponnesian War. Now an exporter of olive oil, rice and cotton, it's an unpretentious but charming small resort. Houses fronted by wrought-iron balconies climb up the lower slopes of 600-foot (186-m.) Mt. Koúmaros. A few ruins can be seen at the top.

Visitors shouldn't miss the action at sunset when the garden square and picturesque quayside are filled with Greeks and tourists gaily streaming in and out of shops or perching at tables by the water to eat the delicious fresh fish. The little island of **Marathonísi** connected to the mainland by a minuscule causeway is graced by a peaceful pine grove, a small white chapel, an ancient tower and a lighthouse. The legend goes that the lovers Paris and Helen spent their first night on

Kranaë, as Homer called the island, after fleeing from Sparta.

Githio's long sand-and-pebble beach north of town is public in theory, but is reached through private land. The Hotel Lakonis in a garden site overlooking the bay welcomes individuals and small groups to its small complex on the beach to use the snack bar and sporting facilities.

The Máni Circuit Tour

You can easily do the circular tour of the Máni (about 160 km.) in a day. Leaving Gíthio, you pass the restored 13th-century crenellated Frankish **Castle of Passavá,** built in 1254 by

Boats glide visitors through the magical caves at Pírgos Diroú.

Jean de Neuilly, Marshal of the Morea and an outstanding military leader. Next—well off the main road—are the remains of the **Kelefá Castle,** a vast 17th-century Turkish fortress.

Areópoli is the small county seat, known for a few bakeries and an 18th-century church (restored from the 11th century) with an apse sculpted with signs of the zodiac.

Pírgos Diroú boasts an underground river of stalactites and stalagmites—a fascinating highlight of the Máni. You can **83**

drive down to the cave entrance from the cliffs above, to make the half-hour visit by flatboat. Discovered in 1895, the caves were opened to the public in 1963. Like the mythical underworld River Styx, it's dark and cool as the boatmen paddle their charges silently along.

It's truly an unforgettable experience, as you view lime-stone formations such as the 400-million-year-old stalagmite, said to be the oldest in the world. Or the "Bridge of Sighs", or "Dracula" and many more. Don't count on a guide speaking English or any other language but Greek.

A small white-rock beach with pellucid waters just a few steps from the grotto makes a relaxing stop for a swim. There's a friendly taverna as well.

As you continue south on the

Váthia's medieval splendour. Right: On the road in the Máni.

circuit, landscapes grow progressively more rugged and villages more deserted—some are simply ruins. Possible stops include CHAROÚDA and GARDENÍTSA, both of which have 11th-century churches and wall paintings of minor interest.

From the fortified village of NÓMIA you can admire a breathtaking **view,** and less noteworthy frescoes in the church. Further along, KÆTA is remarkable for its several typical regional stone watch-towers, but—like most places on this austere coast—the village is almost totally deserted. Nestling in a bay under towering, rocky slopes, **Gerolimín** looks like a sleepy fishing village from the set of a Hollywood film.

On to **Váthia,** where the ghost town full of old dwellings, stony bastions and keeps is being restored to some of its former dignity by the Greek National Tourist Office to attract visitors down to the tip of the Máni.

Beyond PÓRTO KÁGIO is the tip of the peninsula, accessible only on foot. For the return trip you have the choice between the way you came or—past Váthia again—via the eastern coastal road.

This wild, deserted route is on the sunless side of the hills in late afternoon, although the **views** are gorgeous enough, especially from the villages of KOKKÁLA or KÓTRONA. The only road back to Gíthio goes again through Areópoli.

Monemvasía

Rising up from the sea like a fairy-tale vision, Monemvasía will transport you straight back to the Middle Ages. The name comes from the Greek for "only entrance". This fortress-island off the south-east coast of Lakonía can be entered only across a causeway on the foundations of an ancient bridge. The strangely peaceful atmosphere and fantastic scenery really merit a trip here.

Fortified by Byzantium during Slav incursions, Monemvasía was held by the Franks under Guillaume de Villehardouin from 1249 to 1263, when he was obliged to cede it to Michael Paleologos. Venetians and Turks also occupied the fortress at various times. The Franks called it Malvoisie, the English Malmsey, for they loved its celebrated and heady sweet wine.

Today most people stay in the new town opposite the 984-foot (300-m.) fortress rock, but the ancient settlement is what they come to see. The narrow, flower-decked streets—wide enough to be only "sidewalks"—are thronged at times, especially on weekends, but otherwise you'll find them awesomely silent.

Once the town was populated by 30,000 souls, but today only 400 people spend the summer here in restored houses—cave-like and cooling. A few houses may be rented by the day or month, and there's a minute hotel near the main church square.

The largest church, **Elkómenos Christós** (Christ in Chains), in a square with a cannon in front of it, is seen to best advantage during one of the weekend Orthodox services; the priest in silk vestments chants as incense curls upwards and silent women light votive candles.

The main entry door is decorated with a bas-relief of pea-

From ancient bastions you can view the rooftops of Monemvasía.

cocks from the original Byzantine structure; the rest of the church was rebuilt by the Venetians in the 17th century. The barrel-vaulted interior contains some beautiful icons, and you'll see an elaborately carved modern (1974) parade platform for carrying icons during religious festivals.

Monemvasía once had an unbelievable 40 churches. Only a few are left today, as you see when you stroll through the lower town and along its ramparts.

A walk up to the citadel or **Kástro** looks daunting, but is well worth the effort. After ten minutes, you'll reach a series of arched gates, passing through to the old central square, now overgrown with grass, where a couple of large eucalyptus trees provide welcome shade.

From up here the views are magnificent. The town way below looks like a colourful scattering of dolls' houses, and you'll be proud you made the climb.

Further uphill on the cobbled path you reach **Agía Sofía** church, originally Byzantine with an especially elegant brick and stone exterior. Built in the 11th and 12th centuries and partially restored in 1845 and 1970, the church was also used

by Turks as a mosque. Over the portico doors are some remarkable Byzantine marble bas-reliefs.

If you walk just above the church, you gain a grandiose view over the ultramarine sea far below. Rough paths lead to other parts of the large **citadel fortifications.** Constructed as a rectangle with towers at three corners, the original Byzantine citadel was rebuilt several times following various assaults. Not much remains except fragments of the towers.

What to Do

Sports

Active sports enthusiasts will be happy in the Peloponnese if they are good swimmers, sailors, walkers, joggers or mountain climbers. Other sports facilities are limited, though some possibilities do exist.

There are tennis courts at Olympia, Killíni, Pátra and at certain hotels, notably at Río and Kalamáta.

In winter, skiers can indulge in their favourite sport on the slopes of Ostrakína (Ménalo) and Vrissópoulos, both near

Sunning, swimming and windsurfing can be enjoyed on most beaches rimming the Peloponnese.

Olympia and equipped with lifts. The opportunities for hikers are endless. You'll find innumerable shelters in the mountains for more extended hikes.

Water Sports

There's an endless choice of beaches—from private coves away from the mob to vast, sandy strands which might be either crowded or deserted, depending on the place and season.

Countless beaches offer wind-surf boards and pedalos for hire. There are public (government-run) beaches with good facilities at Náfplio and

Pátra. Kyllíni Golden Beach is one of the best around. Apply to the hotel to use its facilities.

The north coast of the Peloponnese has long stretches of mainly pebbly beach; some fully equipped sports centres here hire out water-skiing equipment, wind-surf boards, catamarans and pedalos and provide changing rooms, cafés and tavernas. The west coast from Loutrá Kaiáfas right

All types of boat—pedalo, sailing, motor—are for hire around the coast.

down to Methóni and Koróni boasts sandy beaches and some good swimming. Methóni's sand and rock beach near the old castle is especially appealing.

There's a delightful tiny beach near Pírgos Diroú, not far from the caves on the Máni, but the best beach in the area is undoubtedly at the Lakonis Hotel outside Gíthio. Several first-class hotels, of course, have pools.

Greece is a nation of sailors and you'll find it is the ideal place to go sailing or yachting, island-hopping as you wish. You can rent anything from a dinghy to a fully equipped steamer-sized yacht—that is if you don't have your own. There are several yachting and sailing clubs and schools, including a branch at Pátra.

Underwater Sports

Strict rules regulate the use of scuba apparatus, but it is permitted—from sunrise to sunset, and for viewing fish only—in certain places. Ask at the local tourist office or your hotel if equipment and lessons are available. Spear guns are allowed for hunting small fish.

Snorkelling can be great fun, and the equipment is inexpensive to buy, if you haven't brought your own. Beware of jellyfish—currently the scourge of the Mediterranean.

Fishing

Commercial fishing is a major activity in the Peloponnese, and fortunately the Mediterranean is not yet totally fished out. Apply to the local fishermen to go on board at dawn or later in the day to try your hand. Mainly nets are used. Boats and fishing tackle can also be hired in many ports. Some of the mountain streams have plentiful trout.

Entertainment

Las Vegas it's not, in the quiet Peloponnese. But you will find *bouzoúki* music and sometimes dancing in various tavernas in the larger towns and on the coast. Entertainment is usually an impromptu affair, and musicians make the rounds of the tavernas and cafés.

Discotheques exist in places like Pátra, Kalamáta and Náfplio, and the larger hotels often have discotheques and/or clubs for *sirtáki*—that famous Zorba-style dancing. Courageous spectators are usually invited to join in. It's all very easy-going and relaxed, so knock back your *oúzo* and have fun in the spontaneous Greek manner. **91**

Calendar of Events

Throughout the year in Greece, holidays and religious festivals are celebrated with zest and colour. Some festivals have a local significance, others are observed nationwide.

January 1   Feast of St. Basil. A special "Cake of Kings", *vasilópitta,* is served containing a hidden "good luck" coin.

January 6   Epiphany. The sea, rivers and springs of Greece are blessed by immersing a crucifix in the water.

February   Carnaval. During the three weeks before Lent, masked balls, processions and practical jokes are the order of the day. The most famous celebrations in Greece take place in Pátra.

March/April   Orthodox Good Friday and Easter. Candlelit funeral processions with a flower-bedecked bier pass through the streets at night. Midnight services on Holy Saturday announce Christ is risen. The paschal candle is lighted, church bells peal and fireworks illuminate the sky. Easter Sunday is celebrated with a traditional meal of roast lamb and eggs dyed red.

End May   Paleologia Festival in Mistra. A commemorative mass is held for the Despot Constantine Paleologos.

End June/July   Navy Week. The sea has always played an extremely important role in Greek life. Maritime towns pay tribute to this with revelry and fireworks.

End June to September   Festival of Ancient Drama at Epidauros. On Saturdays and Sundays throughout these months, Classical plays are performed in the ancient theatre.

September 8/9   An anniversary regatta is held in commemoration of the famous naval battle in 1822 when the people of Spétse overcame a superior Ottoman force.

November 30   Feast of St. Andrew. In Pátra, there is a procession in honour of the city's patron saint.

December 24   Christmas Eve. Children—and sometimes adults—sing *kálanda* (Christmas carols) in the streets.

December 31   The old year goes out as gaily as the new year comes in. Children again sing *kálanda* in the streets, presents are exchanged and everyone tries their luck at games of chance.

Shopping

Shopping is an unsophisticated, informal affair in small, friendly shops—department stores and giant supermarkets are rare. Nevertheless, you'll probably find everything you need in most towns.

Pharmacies are well stocked with medicines (including many familiar brands), and sundry items—suntan lotions, cosmetics, insect repellent and so on. Beach towels, straw mats and hats and snorkelling equipment are all readily available and inexpensive, as are batteries and camera supplies (though the latter may cost more than in your own country).

You don't ever bargain in stores selling the above, nor in food or wine shops. Elsewhere bargaining is quite common. Gift

Delicate lace and embroidery is often hand-done by local women.

and souvenir shops usually expect you to discuss the prices they quote and you might get a considerable reduction. Jewellers and rug merchants often give a discount if you buy several items.

Most shops open from 8 a.m. to 1.30 or 2 p.m., Monday to Saturday. Officially they reopen from 5 to 8 p.m. on Tuesday, Thursday and Friday.

Best Buys

Accessories. Some shops sell decorative, supple gold-coloured "woven" or braided wire belts for women that make attractive gifts. Macramé belts and bags can be pretty.

Arts and crafts. Modern artists and artisans live and work in the Peloponnese and nearby islands. You have to look for the "nook and cranny"-style shop selling their work, often worth the price asked. Choose from naive paintings, ceramics, stunning multicoloured ribbon belts, blue hand-blown glass objects, and so on.

Books and music. Museums and archaeological sites sell excellent illustrated books in several languages concentrating on the various regions and artworks. You'll also see beautiful picture books to take home as souvenirs. If you want to remember the sound of the *bouzoúki* or Greek singing, head for the local shop selling records and tapes of Greek music.

Clothing. Lovely crumply and light Egyptian and Greek cottons can be found in shops all over the Peloponnese. You may be attracted by casual pullover or lace-trimmed shirts and blouses, or perhaps easy cotton trousers with drawstrings. Light "oatmeal" pullovers or colourful rough-knit sweaters are specialities to consider.

Food and wine. *Oúzo* makes a nice gift or souvenir (you can buy it duty-free at the airport). The honey is delicious, if you dare carry it home. Dried herbs are presented in little plastic bags weighing next to nothing; Greek oregano and thyme are exquisitely aromatic. Sweet almond and honey cakes also make popular gifts.

Handicrafts. Many shops, especially in Corinth, display a big range of factory-made metal and ceramic goods, modelled after antique pieces on display in local museums. Real antiques are carefully checked by authorities and leave Greece only with permission from the Ministry of Culture.

Jewellery. Look for Byzantine coins framed in gold as pendants; ram's-head rings; dolphin and snake rings and

If it won't all fit into your shopping bag, you can hire a donkey to carry it home.

bracelets; and copies of Mycenaean gold jewellery.

Prices range from negligible to very expensive. Ask for a certificate of authenticity for valuable pieces. All gold and silver articles carry a stamp. Or you can buy imitations, often very pretty and not expensive. Filigree in precious or imitation metals is often displayed.

Rugs. Náfplio, Pátra and the nearby islands, plus some other towns, offer pure wool, hand-woven carpets *(flokáti)* and rugs in traditional patterns.

Shoes. Women's shoes and sandals can be very good buys: shops in Pátra probably offer the widest selection. Men can choose from a wide range of inexpensive sandals, espadrilles and plimsolls (sneakers).

Souvenirs. There's no lack of ideas for gifts and souvenirs. You may find something with an amusing "antique" air— such as a bottle-opener with Alexander's head on it, or pretty salad bowls decorated with graceful Attic maidens. Scarves, T-shirts and other paraphernalia are emblazoned with local names and pictures. **95**

Wining and Dining

Greek food, based on seasonal produce, is simple, colourful and healthy. You can usually count on the freshest vegetables and fruit, from tomatoes and baby marrows (zucchini) to watermelons in the summer. Year-round there's excellent lamb and mutton—and you may well watch the fish you ordered being pulled from the water shortly before it is grilled near your table. The basic ingredients are so good that there is no need to spice them up with fancy sauces.

Meal Times

Greeks eat lunch and dinner very late, although restaurants do serve earlier. Most establishments start to fill up for lunch

Fast food Greek style: hot, grilled corn at a streetside stall.

at 1.30 p.m., but you can go as early as 12.15 or so. The Greeks never sit down to dinner before 9 p.m., but most restaurants serve from 7.30 p.m. onwards.

Where to Eat
You'll find restaurants *(estiatório)* and the less elaborate tavernas all over. In informal places, items on the menu are displayed in a glass counter for you to choose your own fish, chop, vegetable accompaniment. Or else it is quite acceptable to go into the kitchen, peek into the pots and pans simmering on the stove or even into the refrigerator and point out what you would like to eat.

By the sea, you won't have to search out the ideal setting. Diners just drape themselves on chairs with tables teetering at portside and enjoy acceptable to excellent fare. The evening ambience is enchantingly romantic in summer as the moon rises and water slaps gently at the quay and the moored dinghies.

Breakfast
Greeks habitually start the day with nothing more than a few cups of strong, black Greek coffee, plus perhaps some cakes or sweet rolls. Foreigners are given bread, butter and jam with tea or instant coffee.

Juices and fruit are usually available. A few of the larger hotels and cafés propose eggs and bacon or ham, and sometimes cheese and ham on toast.

Appetizers
Greek salad makes a perfect first course—or even a main dish at lunchtime. The sweet tomatoes, onions, olives and cucumber are delicious, and *féta,* white goat's cheese, is added, with a sprinkling of oregano. Salads usually come liberally doused with top-quality olive oil and a bit of vinegar.

But salad every day can be monotonous. Try one of the specialities described below or order a *mezé* platter, a sampling of appetizers.

Dolmádes, vine leaves stuffed with rice and pine-nuts or meat, can be served chilled or hot with lemon sauce.

Dzadzíki combines creamy Greek yoghurt with cucumber and garlic.

Taramosaláta is a mixture of fish roe (usually that of the grey mullet) with mashed potato, oil and seasonings. Lemon and hearty Greek bread come with it.

Melidzanosaláta ("eggplant caviar") is a delicious puree of aubergine, olive oil, garlic and herbs.

Smoked fish sometimes appears on the *mezé* platter.

Soups rarely figure on menus, except for *avgolémono,* a mouthwatering chicken-lemon soup thickened with egg, served hot or cold, or the occasional cold Vichyssoise or cucumber soup.

Hot Snacks

Favourites include spinach pie *(spanakópitta)* and cheese pie *(tiropittákia),* made with the light Greek pastry, *fíllo.* Bite-sized *tirópitta* (cheese-filled pastry) and *pastítsio* (pastry stuffed with spiced chopped meat) make tasty snacks.

Souvláki, skewered pieces of meat or sometimes fish, often with chunks of green peppers and onions, are charcoal-grilled. Meat grilled with fresh vegetables and *dzadzíki* and wrapped in pitta bread is called *souvláki me píta. Donér kebáb* are thin slices of lamb compressed and cooked on a spit, then wrapped in pitta bread and served with tomatoes and onions.

Seafood

You can't do better than to order the excellent fish, shellfish, squid or lobster you'll see temptingly displayed wherever you go. You may be invited to make your choice from a display on ice. Be prepared, though, for reasonably high prices (the price is fixed by weight in grams).

Astakós: clawless "spiny lobster", a sort of large crayfish, is served grilled or boiled, with melted butter or lemon, or sometimes in a salad.

Barboúni: red mullet, considered a delicacy. Usually grilled or fried whole.

Chtapódi: octopus can be marinated and served as a *mezé.* It's also delicious charcoal-grilled or cut in pieces and fried. Although chewy, octopus can taste almost as good as lobster.

Fagrí (sea bream) is usually baked or grilled. *Garídes* (shrimp) may be served in salads or hot. *Glóssa* (sole) is rare, but good when available. *Kéfalos* (grey mullet), *lithríni* (spotted bream), *sinagrída* (red snapper) are all usually grilled whole. *Xifías,* swordfish steaks, are brushed with oil, seasoned with oregano and grilled or cut into pieces and grilled on a skewer.

Meat Dishes

Moussaka *(mousakás),* the national dish, may be eaten for lunch or dinner. Layers of spicy

Greek salad and hunks of bread make simple but delicious fare.

minced lamb or beef alternate with aubergine, the whole topped with a cream sauce *au gratin*. In Corinth they add raisins to the recipe.

Kotópoulo (chicken) generally proves a very good bet since poultry is farm-raised on the Peloponnese. It's usually skewered and grilled with a sprinkling of herbs.

Plain, grilled chops with herbs are delicious. There's abundant lamb, veal and pork. You may also find filet mignon and sirloin steak on the menu, as well as roast pork or lamb.

As an accompaniment you may be offered rice, potatoes *(patátes)*—probably French-fried and often disappointingly limp—or vegetables, whether huge broad beans, white beans, green beans, aubergine, peas, baby marrow or cauliflower.

Desserts

You'll find a tempting selection of fresh fruits, especially in summer. Choose from cherries, watermelons, canteloupe and honeydew melons, pomegranates, strawberries, grapes, peaches, apricots, figs and plums.

Made from goat's milk, Greek yoghurt *(giaoúrti)* has a delicious tang and extraordinary creamy consistancy. Ask for it with honey *(méli)* and

you'll enjoy the food of the gods. *Giaourtokaridómelo* is a long word for a luscious combination of yoghurt, honey and chopped walnuts.

Honey- or syrup-doused pastries such as *baklavás* (pastry, chopped nuts and honey) and *kataífi* (which looks like shredded wheat with nuts and honey) satisfies the Greek sweet tooth. If you get to the island of Spétse, try their almond-cake speciality, *amigdalotá,* a sugar-dusted, buttery treat.

Ices and ice-creams are excellent, made with fresh, honest ingredients, nothing artificial included.

Drinks

Popular (and cheap), perfect in this climate, anis-flavoured *oúzo* is *the* apéritif. Greeks knock it back straight, but you can ask for water and ice. Imported gin, vodka and whisky prove rather expensive. Beer is in good supply, usually a German brand.

Greek wine is plentiful and inexpensive, especially the *retsína,* a dry white wine with a resin flavour. The Peloponnese is the largest wine-growing area in Greece and produces some creditable wines. Nemea is a fruity but dry red and Mavrodafni is a sweet white dessert wine. Some familiar brand names from elsewhere in Greece: Demestica, Cambas, Melsina, Santa Helena—all dry whites, especially good when chilled. Most of the above-mentioned brands come in acceptable dry reds. Other red wines to note are Boutari, Polymenissa (Corfiot), Naoussa (from Páros) and Cava (from northern Greece). Cellar is an easy name to remember, and their white and red wines are both quite good.

Greek brandy, Metaxa, packs a punch and is advertised all over the place.

Greek coffee *(ellinikó kafé)* is a potent brew. Served in a demi-tasse, it comes sweetened (either very sweet, *glikó,* or sweet, *métrio)* or without sugar *(skéto),* according to your stated preference. Coffee is always black, unless you ask for milk *(gála).* A refreshing drink mid-morning or afternoon is *café frappé,* iced coffee with or without cream. The Greeks also drink a lot of instant coffee referred to universally as *nes.* Tea, hot or iced, is always available as well.

Soft drinks and mineral water come in all varieties and flavours.

To Help You Order

Could we have a table?	**The boroúsame na échoume éna trapézi?**
I'd like a/an/some ...	**Tha íthela ...**

beer	**mía bíra**	mineral water	**metallikó neró**
bread	**psomí**		
coffee	**éna kafé**	napkin	**éna trapezomándilo**
cutlery	**macheropírouna**		
		potatoes	**patátes**
dessert	**éna glikó**	rice	**rízi**
fish	**psári**	salad	**mía saláta**
fruit	**froúta**	soup	**mía soúpa**
glass	**éna potíri**	sugar	**záchari**
ice-cream	**éna pagotó**	tea	**éna tsái**
meat	**kréas**	(iced) water	**(pagoméno) neró**
milk	**gála**	wine	**krasí**

101

How to Get There

From Great Britain and Ireland

BY AIR: There are frequent daily non-stop flights to Athens from Heathrow, with connections from other major British and Irish cities via Heathrow. Types of fare: first class, club and economy, as well as eurobudget, excursion, PEX and student. Flying time: approximately 4 hours.

Charter Flights and Package Tours. Athens is a popular destination for charter flights from Great Britain and many tour companies and operators offer seat-only arrangements.

Package tours are available. It is wise to shop around for the best deal. These are usually offered by the specialist Greek tour operators.

BY SEA: In summer, passenger and car ferries operate frequently between certain Italian ports and Greece. The most popular routes are Venice–Pátra and Brindisi–Pátra, though you can also embark at Ancona, Bari and Otranto. You can reach Monemvasía by hydrofoil from Piraeus, and there is a boat from Piraeus that calls in at Monemvasía and Gíthio on its way to Crete.

BY RAIL: You can travel by all the Channel ports and continue by train through Paris, Basle, Zagreb and Belgrade to Athens. From Athens a narrow gauge railway runs round the Peloponnese, stopping at Corinth, Xylocástro, Diakoptó, Pátra, Pírgos, Árgos, Trípoli and Kalamáta.

The other main route down to the Peloponnese is via Paris, Modane and Bologna to Brindisi, from where you can catch the ferry to Pátra (see above).

BY ROAD: At fares only slightly lower than some air tickets, express coach services operate between London and Athens, with a travel time of three days.

For motorists the preferred itinerary is from Dover to either Ostend or Zeebrugge and on to Greece via the motorways skirting Brussels, Munich, Belgrade and Nïs. You can reduce driving time either by loading yourself and your car onto an auto-train for part of the journey (expensive) or by driving through France and Italy and taking one of the Italy–Greece ferries for the final stage of the trip (see above).

From North America

BY AIR: There are direct flights to Athens from New York, Los Angeles, Montreal and Toronto. Types of fare: first class, business and economy, excursion, advance purchase and APEX are available from Canada. From the U.S.A., there are first class, business and economy, military, special economy, APEX, excursion and group fares. Flying time: from New York approximately 11 hours; from Los Angeles approximately 20 hours.

BY SEA: There are passenger-cargo services from Galveston, Houston, New Orleans, New York, Newport News, Baltimore and Charleston to Piraeus.

From Australia

BY AIR: Regular flights go direct from Melbourne and Sydney to Athens. Types of fare: first class, club, economy and one way and round trip excursion. Flying time: from Sydney approximately 23–24 hours.

When to Go

On the whole the Peloponnese enjoys a truly Mediterranean climate with warm to hot days and mild nights. Rainfall and temperatures vary from place to place, but a general guideline would be: blossom season March to June; dry season July to October; rainy season October to March. In the mountainous interior, temperatures are not as high as on the coast and, naturally, there is more snow in winter.

Average daily maximum temperatures:

		J	F	M	A	M	J	J	A	S	O	N	D
Air temperature													
Pátra	°C	14	15	17	20	23	28	31	31	28	24	20	16
(west coast)	°F	57	59	63	68	73	82	88	88	88	75	68	61
Trípoli	°C	9	11	13	18	22	28	31	30	26	22	15	11
(interior)	°F	48	52	55	64	72	82	88	86	79	72	59	52
Water temperature													
Ionian	°C	14	14	14	15	17	21	23	25	23	21	19	16
Sea	°F	57	57	57	59	63	70	73	77	73	70	66	61

Planning Your Budget

To give you an idea of what to expect, here are some average prices in Greek drachmas. Remember that all prices must be regarded as approximate and that inflation is running high.

Baby-sitters. From 400 drs. per hour.

Bicycle hire. From 300 drs. per day.

Camping (per day) 150–180 drs. per person, 65 drs. per car, plus 6% tax.

Car hire (international company, high season, July to September). *Subaru 600* 1,320 drs. per day, 16.80 drs. per km. *Opel Kadett 1.2 S* 2,125 drs. per day, 22.50 drs per km. *BMW 518* 5,300 drs. per day, 51 drs. per km. Add 20% tax. Minimum daily charge 100 km.

Cigarettes. Greek brands 40–65 drs. for a packet of 20, foreign brands 70–100 drs.

Entertainment. *Bouzoúki* (with one drink) from 350 drs., discotheque (with one drink) from 250 drs., cinema 100–200 drs.

Guides. 1,500 drs. for half day, 3,000 drs. for full day.

Hairdressers. *Men's* haircut 200–500 drs. *Women's* haircut 400–800 drs., shampoo and set or blow-dry 500–900 drs., manicure from 400 drs.

Hotels (double room with bath and breakfast). Class A 4,300–4,600 drs., Class B 2,800–3,500 drs., Class C 1,700–2,600 drs., Class D 1,000–1,100 drs. (shared bathroom).

Meals and drinks. Continental breakfast 100–150 drs. Lunch/dinner in fairly good establishment 250–800 drs. Iced coffee 35–50 drs., *oúzo* 50 drs., beer 75 drs., soft drinks 50 drs., whisky-soda or gin-tonic 195 drs.

Shopping bag. Bread (1 kg.) 60–70 drs., butter (250 grams) 75–100 drs., eggs (½ dozen) 60 drs., *féta* cheese (½ kg.) 200–250 drs., potatoes (1 kg.) 40 drs., coffee (½ kg.) 400 drs., soft drinks (small bottle) 35 drs., minced meat (1 kg.) 350–500 drs., beef (1 kg.) 500–700 drs., chicken (1 kg.) 200–250 drs.

Taxis. Meter starts at 20 drs., after that 13.50 drs. per km.

BLUEPRINT for a Perfect Trip

An A-Z Summary of Practical Information and Facts

Contents

A   **AIRPORT** (ΑΕΡΟΔΡΟΜΙΟ—*aerodrómio*). Closest international airport is Athens, 10 km. (6 miles) from the capital. There are two separate terminals reached by different buses: the East Terminal which serves all international airlines except Olympic Airways (the Greek national airline); and the West Terminal which handles only Olympic flights—foreign and domestic. Domestic flights are operated exclusively by Olympic Airways.

Olympic Airways runs a free shuttle service between the two airport terminals every hour from 8 a.m. to 8 p.m.

Both terminals contain offices of the National Tourist Organization (EOT), a currency exchange office, hotel-reservation counters, newsstands, car-hire agencies, refreshment facilities and a duty-free shop. Porters are plentiful.

There's a direct bus service from the airport to the centre of Athens. Coaches leave the East Terminal every 20 minutes from about 6 a.m. to midnight, approximately every hour from midnight to 6 a.m., for Leofóros Amalías 4, just off Síntagma; municipal buses run to Záppio. A West Terminal service leaves for the Olympic town office at Leofóros Singroú 96–100 every half hour (from 6 a.m. to midnight); municipal buses run to Síntagma.

A taxi ride to the centre of Athens takes about 25 minutes.

A few small airports on the Peloponnese serve charters and private planes. Commercial flights run from Athens to Kalamáta once or twice daily (flying time 40 minutes).

Porter!	**Achthofóre!**
Taxi!	**Taxí!**
Where's the bus for ...?	**Pou íne to leoforío giá ...?**

ALPHABET. (See also LANGUAGE, and box on page 30.) The exotic letters of the Greek alphabet needn't be a mystery to you. The table below lists the Greek letters in their capital and small forms, followed by the letters they correspond to in English. In cases where there are various possibilities, we give pronunciation examples.

A	α	a	as in bar		Ξ	ξ	x	like **ks** in thanks
B	β	v			O	o	o	as in bone
Γ	γ	g	as in go*		Π	π	p	
Δ	δ	d	like **th** in this		P	ρ	r	
E	ε	e	as in get		Σ	σ, ς	s	as in kiss
Z	ζ	z			T	τ	t	
H	η	i	like **ee** in meet		Y	υ	i	like **ee** in meet
Θ	θ	th	as in thin		Φ	φ	f	
I	ι	i	like **ee** in meet		X	χ	ch	as in Scottish lo**ch**
K	κ	k			Ψ	ψ	ps	as in ti**psy**
Λ	λ	l			Ω	ω	o	as in bone
M	μ	m			OY	ου	ou	as in soup
N	ν	n						

---

*except before **i**- and **e**-sounds, when it's pronounced like **y** in yes

ANTIQUITIES *(archéa)*. If you find an antiquity, you must report it to the Greek Archaeological Service which may permit you to export it upon payment of a fee. Before you buy an antiquity, make sure that the dealer obtains an export permit for it. Travellers caught trying to smuggle antiquities are subject to prosecution.

Many underwater archaeological sites have been declared off-limits to amateur divers (but not snorkellers), with penalties decreed for anyone even touching an antiquity at such places.

Greek Archaeological Service: Polignótou 13, Athens

BEACHES. The National Tourist Organization runs a certain number of organized public beaches. These offer facilities such as changing rooms, restaurants and snack bars, shops, children's playgrounds, tennis courts, pedalos, etc. They charge minimal entry fees. The largest public beaches are Arvanitiá at Náfplio and Pátra Beach. You'll find public and semi-public beaches everywhere, but take care; life-guard surveillance is minimal in most places. The longest stretch of sandy beach is on the west coast between Pírgos and Filiatrá.

C CAMPING* (ΚΑΜΠΙΝΓΚ—"*camping*"). Camping in Greece is permitted only at organized sites; there's no lack of these throughout the area. Campers will be impressed by the space, shade and cleanliness of the sites, as well as by the imagination that has gone into providing facilities.

The National Tourist Organization runs two large campsites in the Peloponnese: Pátron Camping, 5 km. (3 miles) from Pátra, and Killíni Camping at Loutrá Killínis, near Vartholomió on the west coast. There are also more than 60 privately run campsites on the peninsula, licensed by the National Tourist Organization.

Is there a campsite near by?	**Ipárchi éna méros giá "camping" edó kondá?**

CAR HIRE* (ΕΝΟΙΚΙΑΣΕΙΣ ΑΥΤΟΚΙΝΗΤΩΝ —*enikiásis-aftokiníton*). (See also DRIVING IN GREECE.) Athens is the best place to hire a car, as all major agencies are located there, but you can also hire one in Pátra. Prices are high, as everywhere in Greece. All types of car are available. There are few air-conditioned models, and automatic gear-shift is the exception rather than the rule. You should request these in advance.

Officially an International Driving Permit is obligatory for all foreigners *hiring* a car in Greece, but in practice firms accept virtually any national licence, stipulating that it must have been held for at least one year. To be safe, you should obtain an International Permit from your motoring association before leaving. A firm may well insist that the driver be 25. Deposits are normally waived for credit card holders.

The rates on page 104 include only third-party insurance and are subject to a tax. Off-season prices are 10 to 20% lower.

I'd like to hire a car (tomorrow).	**Tha íthela na nikiáso éna aftokínito (ávrio).**
for one day/a week	**giá mía iméra/mía evdomáda**
Please include full insurance.	**Sas parakaló na simberilávete miktí asfália.**

CHILDREN. The Peloponnese is wonderful for youngsters, especially around the beaches, but keep a close eye on your own. Greek children learn to swim at a very early age and are fearless in the water.

If you need a baby-sitter, enquire at the hotel reception desk, and arrangements will be made, providing you give sufficient warning (a day or two ahead, usually).

If your child wanders off, ask around (anybody who speaks your language), and if you don't get results within a few minutes, go to the police or any type of supervisor nearby (beach attendants, hotel desks). It's unlikely any harm will come to your child in Greece.

Can you get me a baby-sitter for tonight?	**Boríte na mou vríte mía "baby-sitter" giapópse?**

CIGARETTES, CIGARS, TOBACCO* *(tsigára, poúra, kapnós).* The sign to look for is ΚΑΠΝΟΠΩΛΕΙΟ *(kapnopolío).* Greek tobacco products, of good quality and generally mild, are far cheaper than the foreign brands (some manufactured under licence in Greece) available. These may be hard to obtain, so buy supplies duty-free in your country (see CUSTOMS AND ENTRY REGULATIONS).

A packet of .../A box of matches, please.	**Éna pakéto .../Éna koutí spírta, parakaló.**
filter-tipped	**me fíltro**
without filter	**chorís fíltro**

CLIMATE and CLOTHING. You'll need informal, light clothing in the summer (cotton is much the coolest), warmer clothing in the winter, when temperatures drop and it can rain heavily at times. In summer don't forget beachwear, sunglasses, a hat and perhaps beach shoes for rough and rocky terrain or protection against sea-urchins. Sturdy espadrilles or walking shoes are necessary for some of the climbing and scrambling around ancient sites.

For evenings you may want to dress up a bit, especially in the more expensive hotels; skirts or smart trousers for women, nice sports shirts and maybe a jacket for men. Women should have a skirt handy for visiting monasteries. Take a light wrap or sweater even in summer since cool breezes can blow up, especially in June and September.

The Greeks themselves don't go in for nude or topless bathing, but topless is becoming more acceptable for foreigners, and though nudism is illegal, it does exist on the islands and in isolated places.

COMMUNICATIONS

Post offices (ΤΑΧΥΔΡΟΜΕΙΟ—*tachidromío*) handle letters, stamp sales, parcels and money orders, but not telegrams and phone calls. They can be recognized by a yellow sign reading ΕΛ.ΤΑ.

C **Hours** are usually from 8 a.m. to 8 p.m., Monday to Saturday.

In tourist hotels, the reception desk will usually take care of despatching mail.

Registered letters and parcels going out of Greece are checked before being sent, so don't seal them until you have presented them at the post office desk.

Poste restante (general delivery). If you don't know ahead of time where you'll be staying, address your mail *Poste Restante*. You can collect your mail at the town's main post office. Take your passport or identity card with you.

Telegrams *(tilegráfima)* **and telephone** *(tiléfono)*. Every town of any size has an office of the Greek Telecommunications Organization—OTE—and this is where you go to telephone or send telegrams—if, that is, your hotel does not provide these facilities. Tourist hotel staff are very helpful and, as well as putting your call in for you, take telephone messages and handle telex communications.

Where's the (nearest) post office?	**Pou íne to kodinótero tachidromío?**
Have you received any mail for …?	**Échete grámmata giá …?**
A stamp for this letter/ postcard, please.	**Éna grammatósimo giaftó to grámma/kart postál, parakaló.**
express (special delivery)	**exprés**
airmail	**aeroporikós**
registered	**sistiméno**
I want to send a telegram to …	**Thélo na stílo éna tilegráfima sto …**
Can you get me this number in …?	**Boríte na mou párete aftó ton arithmó …?**
reverse-charge (collect) call	**plirotéo apóton to paralípti**
person-to person (personal) call	**prosopikí klísi**

COMPLAINTS. Either the proprietor of the establishment in question or your hotel manager, travel-agency representative or tour operator should be the first recourse for complaints. If you still aren't satisfied, go to the tourist police (see POLICE). Simply mentioning you intend doing so should bring results. Many disputes stem from small misunderstandings or linguistic problems. Rather than explode in anger, draw a deep breath and try to see things the Greek way—especially where time is involved.

CONSULATES and EMBASSIES *(proxenío; presvía)*. Embassies of all major countries are located in Athens. However, as a foreign tourist with problems, you'll want to contact your consular representative, not your embassy—though they may often be found in the same building. Hours vary so it's best to call first.

Australia:	Leofóros Mesogíon 15; tel.: 3604-611/15.
Canada:	Gennadíou 4/Ipsilántou; tel.: 7239-511.
Eire:	Leofóros Vas. Konstantínou 7; tel.: 7232-771.
Great Britain:	Ploutárchou 1/Ipsilántou, Athens; tel. 7236-211.
	2, Vódzi Street, Pátra; tel. 277-329.
New Zealand:	An. Tsócha 15–17, Ambelokípi; tel.: 6410-311.
South Africa:	Leofóros Kifisías 124; tel.: 6922-125.
U.S.A.:	Leofóros Vas. Sofías 91; tel.: 7212-951.

CONVERSION CHARTS. For fluid and distance measures, see page 114. Greece uses the metric system.

Temperature

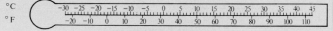

Length

Weight

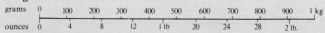

COURTESIES. (See also MEETING PEOPLE.) People in the Peloponnese are friendly, kind and relaxed, and they'll make a big effort to help you, especially if you're in trouble. They're easy to talk to, even if your Greek is minimal and they don't speak your language. Sign language usually does it. Most people are quite happy to be photographed, although it's always polite to ask permission in advance.

Social conventions are quite strictly observed. A handshake is normal when meeting and parting from a friend. Shopkeepers expect

C a "good morning" (or "good afternoon") and a "goodbye" (see
LANGUAGE).

Greeks wish each other "bon appétit" before a meal. In Greek, the
expression is *kalí órexi*. A common toast when drinking is *stin igiá
sas,* meaning "cheers". A reply to any toast, *epísis,* means "the same
to you". It is not considered good manners to fill a wine glass nor to
drain it completely. The custom is to keep it topped up.

Don't show the palms of your hands when waving. This gesture is
known as *moúndza* and considered offensive, especially in out-of-the-
way places. Learn to wave in regal fashion with the palm towards you.

CRIME and THEFT. Honesty is a matter of pride. Any idea of
stealing from a guest is thoroughly repellent to the people of this
hospitable nation. Nevertheless, common sense suggests you keep an
eye on things and confide valuables to the hotel reception.

You should keep in mind that possession of narcotics is a serious
matter in Greece.

CUSTOMS and ENTRY REGULATIONS. (See also DRIVING IN
GREECE.)

The following chart shows what main duty-free items you may take
into Greece and, upon your return home, into your own country:

Into:	Cigarettes		Cigars		Tobacco	Spirits		Wine
Greece 1)	300	or	75	or	400 g.	1½ l.	or	4 l.
2)	200	or	50	or	250 g.	1 l.	or	2 l.
Australia	200	or	250 g.	or	250 g.	1 l.	or	1 l.
Canada	200	and	50	and	900 g.	1.1 l.	or	1.1 l.
Eire	300	or	75	or	400 g.	1½ l.	and	3 l.
N. Zealand	200	or	50	or	½ lb.	1 qt.	and	1 qt.
S. Africa	400	and	50	and	250 g.	1 l.	and	1 l.
U.K.	200	or	50	or	250 g.	1 l.	and	2 l.
U.S.A.	200	and	100	or	3)	1 l.	or	1 l.

1) Passengers arriving from EEC countries.
2) Passengers arriving from other countries.
3) A reasonable quantity.

Visitors from EEC (Common Market) countries only need an identity card to enter Greece. Citizens of most other countries must be in possession of a valid passport. European and North American residents are not subject to any health requirements. In case of doubt, check with Greek representatives in your own country before departure.

Currency restrictions. Foreign visitors to Greece are not allowed to take into or out of the country more than 3,000 drachmas in local currency. There's no limit on the foreign currency or traveller's cheques you may import or export as a tourist, though amounts in excess of $500 or its equivalent must be declared to the customs official upon arrival.

| I've nothing to declare. | **Den écho na dilóso típota.** |
| It's for my personal use. | **Íne giá prosopikí chrísi.** |

DRIVING IN GREECE

Entering Greece: To bring your car into Greece you'll need:

International Driving Permit (see below)	car registration papers	Green Card (an extension to your regular insurance policy, making it valid for foreign countries)
	nationality plate or sticker	

Foreign visitors driving their own car in Greece need an International Driving Permit, except for nationals of Great Britain, Belgium, Holland, West Germany, Austria and Switzerland. The permit can be obtained through your home motoring association or through the Greek Automobile and Touring Club (E.L.P.A.) on presentation of your national licence, your passport and two photographs.

If you don't have a Green Card, you'll be required to take out Greek insurance at your point of entry.

The standard European red warning triangle is required in Greece for emergencies. Seat belts are obligatory. Motorcycle riders and their passengers must wear crash helmets.

Speed limits are 100 kilometres per hour (62 m.p.h.) on motorways (expressways), 80 k.p.h. (50 m.p.h.) on country roads and 50 k.p.h. (31 m.p.h.) in towns.

Driving conditions. Traffic keeps to the right. All major roads in the Peloponnese are asphalted. Some roads are deceptively "good", and

D you may suddenly run into a rough, unpaved spot just around the corner—or what looks like a gentle curve may be more like a hairpin bend. Falling rocks are another hazard, as are flocks of goats or sheep. Observe utmost caution at all times, especially since Greek drivers range from the prudent to the eccentric. Remember that you don't know the roads here. The biggest highway in the region is the road from Athens to Pátra. It's not quite a motorway (expressway), but a nominal toll is charged. Slower drivers are expected to keep to the far right.

Traffic lights are few and far between in the Peloponnese, except in Pátra. But observe crossroads carefully and watch out for one-way streets.

Parking. In most places you'll find it fairly easy to park your car. But be very careful in crowded areas, such as Pátra, where your car may be towed away if you're parked in an illegal zone. In Náfplio you cannot park in the old part of town (there's a parking lot near the harbour).

Fuel and oil. Service stations are in ample supply, but when you're travelling in rather deserted areas such as Messinía and the Máni, be sure to keep your fuel supply quite high. Petrol stations are usually indicated in advance by a sign showing a tank.

Note that the majority of service stations close at 7 p.m. or earlier (especially at weekends). Only a few stay open in turns after that hour. Fuel prices are among Europe's highest.

Fluid measures

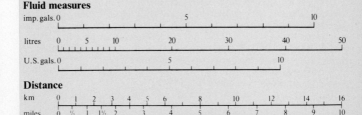

Breakdowns. Breakdown assistance is offered by the Automobile Association of Greece (E.L.P.A.) whose patrol network covers all the main highways of the mainland. Their vehicles bear the sign: "O.V.E.L.P.A."/"Assistance Routière A.T.C.C."/"Road Assistance". Telephone 104 for on-the-spot help.

E.L.P.A. has headquarters in Árgos, Corinth, Kalamáta, Pátra and Trípoli. Signs in these towns clearly indicate the way.

Road signs. Most road signs feature the standard pictographs used throughout Europe. However, you may encounter these written signs:

ΑΛΙΕΞΟΔΟΣ	No through road
ΑΛΤ	Stop
ΑΝΩΜΑΛΙΑ ΟΔΟΣΤΡΩΜΑΤΟΣ	Bad road surface
ΑΠΑΓΟΡΕΥΕΤΑΙ Η ΑΝΑΜΟΝΗ	No waiting
ΑΠΑΓΟΡΕΥΕΤΑΙ Η ΕΙΣΟΔΟΣ	No entry
ΑΠΑΓΟΡΕΥΕΤΑΙ Η ΣΤΑΘΜΕΥΣΙΣ	No parking
ΔΙΑΒΑΣΙΣ ΠΕΖΩΝ	Pedestrian crossing
ΕΛΑΤΤΩΣΑΤΕ ΤΑΧΥΤΗΤΑΝ	Reduce speed
ΕΠΙΚΙΝΔΥΝΟΣ ΚΑΤΩΦΕΡΕΙΑ	Dangerous incline
ΕΡΓΑ ΕΠΙ ΤΗΣ ΟΔΟΥ	Roadworks in progress (Men working)
ΚΙΝΔΥΝΟΣ	Caution
ΜΟΝΟΔΡΟΜΟΣ	One-way traffic
ΠΑΡΑΚΑΜΠΤΗΡΙΟΣ	Diversion (Detour)
ΠΟΔΗΛΑΤΑΙ	Cyclists
ΠΟΡΕΙΑ ΥΠΟΧΡΕΩΤΙΚΗ ΔΕΞΙΑ	Keep right
ΣΤΑΣΙΣ ΛΕΩΦΟΡΕΙΟΥ	Bus stop

(International) Driving Licence	**(diethnís) ádia odigíseos**
car registration papers	**ádia kikloforías**
Green Card	**asfália aftokinítou**
Can I park here?	**Boró na stathméfso edó?**
Are we on the right road for ...?	**Ímaste sto sostó drómo giá ...?**
Full tank, please—	**Na to gemísete me venzíni**
normal/super.	**aplí/soúper, parakaló.**
Check the oil/tires/battery.	**Na elénxete ta ládia/ta lásticha/ ti bataría.**
I've had a breakdown.	**Épatha mía vlávi.**
There's been an accident.	**Égine éna distíchima.**

ELECTRIC CURRENT. The standard current is 220-volt, 50-cycle A.C. Sockets are either two- or three-pin.

I need an adaptor/a battery, please.	**Chriázome éna metaschimatistí/ mía bataría, parakaló.**

E   **EMERGENCIES.** The following numbers are the ones to call in case of emergency.

Police emergency squad	100
Fire	199

Depending on the nature of the emergency, refer also to the separate entries in this section such as CONSULATES AND EMBASSIES, MEDICAL CARE, POLICE.

These words are handy to know in difficult situations:

Careful	**Prosochí**	Police	**Astinomía**
Help	**Voíthia**	Stop	**Stamatíste**

G   **GUIDES and INTERPRETERS*** *(xenagós; diermínéas)*. Guides from tour agencies accompany groups to the main archaeological sites. They speak several major European languages. If you want a personal guide you should enquire at the tourist office or at a tour agency.

We'd like an English-speaking guide.	**Tha thélame éna xenagó pou na milá i angliká.**
I need an English interpreter.	**Chriázome éna ánglo diermínéa.**

H   **HAIRDRESSERS** (ΚΟΜΜΩΤΗΡΙΟ—*kommotírio*) **and BARBERS*** (ΚΟΥΡΕΙΟ—*kourío*). You can expect intense and genuine personal interest not only in your hair, but also in yourself. Hairdressers are delightfully friendly, but don't expect them to be fast.

The following vocabulary will help:

I'd like a shampoo and set.	**Thélo loúsimo ke miz-an-plí.**
I want a ...	**Thélo ...**
haircut	**koúrema**
blow-dry (brushing)	**chténisma me to pistoláki**
permanent wave	**permanád**
colour chart	**éna digmatológio**
colour rinse	**mía dekolorasión**
manicure	**manikioúr**
Don't cut it too short.	**Mi ta kópsete polí kondá.**
A little more off (here).	**Lígo pió kondá (edó).**

HITCH-HIKING *(oto-stóp)*. In a country where human contact is
116 valued, it is considered perfectly normal to give a lift, or to ask for

one. Needless to say, caution about whom you travel with is always
wise.

Can you give me/us a lift to ...?   **Boríte na me/mas páte méchri to ...?**

HOTELS and ACCOMMODATION* (ΞΕΝΟΔΟΧΕΙΟ ΔΩΜΑΤΙΑ—
xenodochío; domátia). (See also CAMPING.) Accommodation ranges
from luxury hotels to modest rooms in private houses. If you arrive
without a reservation, contact the EOT (National Tourist Office)
reception desk at Athens airport or in Pátra (see TOURIST INFORMA-
TION OFFICES). Local tourist police will also advise on accommodation
in the area.

There are youth hostels at Mycenae, Náfplio, Olympia and Pátra.

I'd like a single/double room.   **Tha íthela éna monó/dipló domátio.**

with bath/shower   **me bánio/dous**

What's the rate per night?   **Piá íne i timí giá mía níkta?**

LANGUAGE. (See also ALPHABET and box on page 30.) Some Greeks
have worked in Germany, Australia or the United States and speak
German or English. Some speak French. Nevertheless you'll often
meet Greeks who speak only their own language. The Berlitz phrase
book GREEK FOR TRAVELLERS covers most of the situations you are
likely to encounter.

The Greeks themselves actually have two languages—the classical
katharévousa, until recently the language of the courts and parliament
and still used by a few conservative newspapers, and *dimotikí,* the
spoken language and now also the official one. This is what you'll
hear in Greece today.

The following phrases are ones you'll want to use often:

Good morning	**Kaliméra**	Please	**Parakaló**
Good afternoon	**Kalispéra**	Thank you	**Efcharistó**
Good night	**Kaliníkta**	Goodbye	**Chérete**

Do you speak English?   **Miláte angliká?**
I don't speak Greek.   **Den miló elliniká.**

LAUNDRY and DRY-CLEANING (ΠΛΥΝΤΗΡΙΟ—*plintírio;* ΚΑΘΑ-
ΡΙΣΤΗΡΙΟ—*katharistírio*). In this climate it's easy to rinse out small
articles yourself. They dry in just a few hours.

L

During the peak season, allow three or four days for hotel laundry and dry-cleaning services. You'll find it quicker and cheaper to go to the local laundry, but colours may come back faded.

Where's the nearest laundry/ dry-cleaners?	**Pou íne to kodinótero plintírio/ katharistírio?**
When will it be ready?	**Póte tha íne étimo?**
I must have this for tomorrow morning.	**Prépi na íne étimo ávrio to proí.**

LOST PROPERTY. If you lose something, you have a good chance of getting it back. While there aren't lost property offices in the Peloponnese, in all likelihood anything lost will be turned in at the local police station, or kept in the place where you left it. Otherwise contact the local tourist police.

I've lost my wallet/handbag/ passport.	**Échasa to portofóli mou/tin tsánda mou/to diavatírio mou.**

M

MAPS. The National Tourist Organization (EOT) provides simplified, accurate maps of various parts of the region in their tourist brochures, with street- and place-names given in the Roman alphabet. These are also available at most hotel reception desks. The maps in this book are by Falk-Verlag, Hamburg.

I'd like a street plan of ...	**Tha íthela éna odikó chárti tou**
a road map of this region	**éna chárti aftís tis periochís**

MEDICAL CARE. It is sensible to take out health insurance covering the risk of illness or accident while you're on holiday. Your insurance representative or travel agent at home will be able to advise you best. On the spot, you can turn to a Greek insurance company for coverage corresponding to your requirements and length of stay. Emergency treatment is free, but if you have an insurance you'll enjoy better medical care in the case of hospitalization. British citizens are entitled to the same health cover as the Greeks, but they should apply to the Department of Health and Social Security for a special form before leaving the U.K.

The two main tourist afflictions are sunburn and minor stomach upsets. Work on your suntan gradually, using strong sun-filter creams during the first days and avoiding the midday sun. Wear a hat and sunglasses. If you should step on a sea urchin or get stung by a jellyfish while bathing, apply lemon juice or olive oil for the sea-urchin splinter; ammonia for jellyfish bites can be bought in a stick. Moderation in eating and drinking should see you over the change of diet; any serious problems lasting more than a day or so require a doctor's attention. Bring a reasonable supply of your favourite remedies and necessary medicines from home in case they are not available here.

Pharmacies (ΦAPMAKEIO—*farmakío*) are easily recognized by the sign outside—a red cross on a white background. Chemists take turns in offering a 24-hour service. The address of the chemist on duty will be posted on all pharmacy doors.

Pharmacists can generally advise on minor problems such as cuts, sunburn, blisters, throat infections and gastric disorders.

Where's the nearest (all-night) pharmacy?	**Pou íne to kodinótero (dianikterévon) farmakío?**
I need a doctor/dentist.	**Chriázome éna giatró/ odontogiatró.**
an ambulance	**éna asthenofóro**
hospital	**nosokomío**
sunstroke	**ilíasi**
a fever	**piretós**
an upset stomach	**varistomachiá**

MEETING PEOPLE. It's quite easy to meet people—Greek or otherwise—in the Peloponnese, since most places tourists visit are relaxed and holiday-style. You can strike up a conversation in shops, restaurants, when visiting ruins or wherever you are.

It's easy to make friends of all ages on the beach. Incidentally, a tradition exists for getting to know foreigners who aren't sun-tanned, since they have obviously just arrived and are likely to be around for a while. The sun-tanned ones, on the other hand, are probably about to pack their bags!

How do you do?	**Ti kánete?**
How are you?	**Pos íste?**
Very well, thank you.	**Polí kalá, efcharistó.**

MONEY MATTERS

Currency *(nómisma)*. Greece's monetary unit is the drachma (*drachmí* abbreviated drs.—in Greek, Δρχ.).

Coins: 1, 2, 5, 10, 20, 50 drachmas.
The old (pre-1976) coinage is no longer accepted.
Banknotes: 50, 100, 500, 1,000 and 5,000 drachmas.

M **Banks and currency-exchange offices** (ΤΡΑΠΕΖΑ—*trápeza;* ΣΥΝ-ΑΛΛΑΓΜΑ—*sinállagma*). Banking hours are from 8 a.m. to 2 p.m. Monday to Friday.

Major hotels change money, but at a slightly less advantageous rate than banks. Take your passport as identification.

Credit cards and traveller's cheques *(pistotikí kárta; "traveller's cheque")*. Internationally known credit cards are honoured in most shops (indicated by a sign in the window) and by all banks, car hire firms and leading hotels. Traveller's cheques, widely accepted, are best cashed at a bank (remember your passport for identification).

Paying cash. You may be able to pay for goods in some places with foreign currency, but paying in drachmas is less trouble for everybody.

I want to change some pounds/ dollars.	**Thélo na alláxo merikés líres/ meriká dollária.**
Do you accept traveller's cheques?	**Pérnete "traveller's cheques"?**
Can I pay with this credit card?	**Boró na plíroso me aftí tin pistotikí kárta?**

N **NEWSPAPERS and MAGAZINES** *(efimerída; periodikó)*. Most foreign dailies—including the principal British newspapers and the Paris-based *International Herald Tribune*—appear on news-stands the day following publication. There is a good selection of foreign magazines from most European countries.

Have you any English-language newspapers?	**Échete anglikés efimerídes?**

P **PHOTOGRAPHY.** A photo shop is advertised by the sign ΦΩΤΟΓ-ΡΑΦΕΙΟ *(fotografío)*. Leading brands of film are usually available in the Peloponnese. Black-and-white film is processed in a couple of days, but colour slides and colour film will take one to two weeks. Hand-held cameras may be used in some, but not all, museums and at archaeological sites. The complicated restrictions on use of tripods and cine-filming are not always strictly applied. For security reasons it is illegal to use a tele-photo lens aboard an aircraft. Military sites are, of course, forbidden to photographers and are marked accordingly.

I'd like some film for this camera.	**Tha íthela éna film giaftí ti michaní.**

black-and-white film	**asprómavro film**
colour prints	**énchromo film**
colour slides	**énchromo film giá sláids**
35-mm film	**éna film triánda pénde milimétr**
super-8	**soúper-októ**

| How long will it take to develop (and print) this film? | **Se póses iméres boríte na emfanísete (ke na ektipósete) aftó to film?** |

| May I take a picture? | **Boró na páro mía fotografía?** |

POLICE *(astinomía)*. Regular policemen are called *chorofílakes*. You'll recognize them by their grey-green uniforms.

The tourist police *(touristikí astinomía)* are a separate branch of the police force whose job it is to help foreign visitors in distress. The national flag emblems sewn on their grey uniforms indicate which foreign languages they speak.

In the Peloponnese, there are tourist police for instance in:

Corinth	tel. (0741) 42258	Pírgos	tel. (0621) 23685
Kalamáta	tel. (0721) 23187	Sparta	tel. (0731) 28671
Olympia	tel. (0624) 22550	Trípoli	tel. (071) 223039

PUBLIC HOLIDAYS *(argíes)*. Banks, offices and shops are closed throughout Greece on the following civil and religious holidays:

Jan. 1	*Protochroniá*	New Year's Day
Jan. 6	*ton Theofaníon*	Epiphany
March 25	*Ikostí Pémti Martíou (tou Evangelismoú)*	Greek Independence Day
May 1	*Protomagiá*	May Day
Aug. 15	*Dekapendávgoustos (tis Panagías)*	Assumption Day
Oct. 28	*Ikostí Ogdói Oktovríou*	*Óchi* ("No") Day, commemorating Greek defiance of Italian ultimatum and invasion of 1940
Dec. 25	*Christoúgenna*	Christmas Day
Dec. 26	*défteri iméra ton Christougénnon*	St. Stephen's Day

121

P

Movable dates:	*Katharí Deftéra*	1st Day of Lent: Clean Monday
	Megáli Paraskeví	Good Friday
	Deftéra tou Páscha	Easter Monday

Note: The dates on which the movable holy days are celebrated often differ from those in the West.

Are you open tomorrow? **Échete aniktá ávrio?**

R **RADIO and TV** *(rádio; tileórasi)*. The Greek National Radio (ERT) broadcasts the news and weather in English early in the morning.

On short-wave bands, reception of the World Service of the BBC is extremely clear. Voice of America's English programmes are also easily picked up.

Most hotels, and some bars and restaurants have TV lounges. Many of the programmes are well-known TV series in English with Greek subtitles.

S **SIGHTSEEING TOURS.** Agencies organize tours of the Peloponnese from Athens lasting from one to nine days. A typical one-day trip takes in Corinth, Mycenae, Árgos, Náfplio, Epidaurus. The comprehensive six-day tour covers some 25 different spots. The nine-day trip features the highlights of the Peloponnese, but also takes in Delphi, Salonica and many other parts of the mainland.

Several one-day tours from Kalamáta take in various nearby sights. From Náfplio there are half-day trips to Epidauros alone; or to Epidauros, Mycenae, Árgos and Tiryns. There are also day tours of Náfplio and to Mistra-Sparta.

T **TIME DIFFERENCES.** The chart below shows the time difference between Greece and various cities. In summer, Greek clocks are put forward one hour.

	New York	London	**Athens**	Jo'burg	Sydney	Auckland
winter:	5 a.m.	10 a.m.	**noon**	noon	9 p.m.	11 p.m.
summer:	5 a.m.	10 a.m.	**noon**	11 a.m.	7 p.m.	9 p.m.

122 What time is it? **Ti óra íne?**

TIPPING. By law, service charges are included in the bill at hotels, restaurants and tavernas. The Greeks aren't tip-crazy, but they do expect you to leave a little more—if the service has been good, of course. Around Christmas and Easter, restaurant service charges are increased by a certain percentage and taxis also charge extra. In bars and cafés you should leave an extra 5% at these times of year.

Even if your room or meals are included as part of a package tour, you'll still want to remember the maid and the waiter. The waiter will probably have a *mikró* (an assistant, or busboy), who should get a token of appreciation as well.

Hotel porter, per bag	30–50 drs.
Maid, per day	50 drs.
Waiter	5% (optional)
Taxi driver	10% (optional)
Tourist guide	100–200 drs. (optional)
Hairdresser/Barber	10%
Lavatory attendant	20 drs.

TOILETS (ΤΟΥΑΛΕΤΤΕΣ—*toualéttes*). There are usually centrally located public facilities in the main towns, marked ΓΥΝΑΙΚΩΝ (ladies) and ΑΝΔΡΩΝ (gentlemen).

Where are the toilets?   **Pou íne i toualéttes?**

TOURIST INFORMATION OFFICES *(grafío pliroforión tourismoú)*. The following branches of the National Tourist Office of Greece will supply you with a wide range of colourful and informative brochures and maps in English:

British Isles. 195-7, Regent St., London W1R 8DL.; tel. (01) 734-5997

U.S.A. 645 5th Ave., New York, NY 10022; tel. (212) 421-5777; 611W. 6th St., Los Angeles, CA 90017; tel. (213) 626-6696; 168 N. Michigan Ave., Chicago, IL 60601; tel. 641-6600, 782-1084

Canada. 2, place Ville Marie, Suite 67, Esso Plaza, Montreal, Que., H3B 2C9; tel. (514) 871-1535

T The central headquarters of the National Tourist Organization (*Ellinikós Organismós Tourismoú,* abbreviated EOT) is in Athens: Amerikís 2; tel. (01) 322-3111/9.

EOT has a branch in Pátra:

Iróon Politechníou, Glifáda, Pátra; tel. (061) 420305.

TRANSPORT

Boat. From Piraeus there are ferries to Náfplio (daily in summer), Leonídio (daily in summer; twice weekly in winter) and Monemvasía (daily in summer, four times weekly in winter).

Río is connected to Antírio on the mainland by ferry every 15 minutes, Égio to Ágios Nikólaos several times daily. Zákinthos can be reached by ferry three or four times daily from Killíni; the trip takes 1½ hours.

The Saronic Islands (Póros, Spétse, Hydra) can be reached from both the Peloponnese and Athens by various types of boat. Hydrofoil is the fastest.

Bus. Bus is the best way to travel in the Peloponnese. Even the smallest towns can be reached by bus, although service is not so frequent. To find out about schedules, go to one of the larger bus stations: Athens, Pátra, Náfplio, Sparta, Kalamáta, Corinth. Buses are inexpensive, usually hot and crowded. But the scenery is lovely, and at least you're not driving!

There are also frequent bus services between Athens and towns in the Peloponnese. Buses leave from the railway station, Stathmós Peloponnísou. The trip from Athens to Corinth takes 1½ hours, to Pátra, 3½ hours. ΣΤΑΣΙΣ *(stásis)* is the bus-stop sign.

Taxi. You'll find taxis in many of the larger towns. They're relatively cheap and convenient. If there's no meter, agree on a price before you set off. If you're satisfied, you may add a small tip or about 10% of your fare. There may be charges added on for luggage, late-night service, waiting and on special holidays.

Train. There are narrow-gauge train lines covering the northern and western coasts from Athens through Corinth, Pátra, down to Kiparissía and Kalamáta, with a connection to Olympia. Another line traverses the central part of the Peloponnese from Corinth to Kalamáta, via Árgos and Trípoli. Train travel is inexpensive and sometimes quite scenic, but the service is neither very rapid nor extensive.

In Athens, the station for trains to the Peloponnese is Stathmós Peloponnísou, north-west of the city centre.

Where's the railway station/ the nearest bus stop?	**Pou íne o sidirodromikós stathmós/o kodinóteros stathmós ton leoforíon?**
When's the next boat/bus/ train to ...	**Póte févgi to epómeno plío/leoforío/tréno giá ...?**
I want a ticket to ...	**Thélo éna isitírio giá ...**
single (one-way)	**apló**
return (round-trip)	**me epistrofí**
first/second class	**próti/deftéra thési**
Will you tell me when to get off?	**Tha mou píte pou na katevó?**
Where can I get a taxi?	**Pou boró na vro éna taxí?**
What's the fare to ...?	**Piá íne i timí giá ...?**

WATER *(neró).* Tap water is safe to drink. Bottled mineral water is also available.

a bottle of mineral water	**éna boukáli metallikó neró**
fizzy (carbonated)/still	**me/chorís anthrakikó**

NUMBERS

0	midén		18	dekaoktó
1	éna		19	dekaenniá
2	dío		20	íkosi
3	tría		21	íkosi éna
4	téssera		22	íkosi dío
5	pénde		30	triánda
6	éxi		31	triánda éna
7	eptá		40	saránda
8	októ		50	penínda
9	enniá		60	exínda
10	déka		70	evdomínda
11	éndeka		80	ogdónda
12	dódeka		90	enenínda
13	dekatría		100	ekató
14	dekatéssera		101	ekatón éna
15	dekapénde		102	ekatón dío
16	dekaéxi		500	pendakósia
17	dekaeptá		1,000	chília

SOME USEFUL EXPRESSIONS

yes/no	**ne/óchi**
please/thank you	**parakaló/efcharistó**
excuse me/you're welcome	**me sinchoríte/tipota**
where/when/how	**pou/póte/pos**
how long/how far	**póso keró/póso makriá**
yesterday/today/tomorrow	**chthes/símera/ávrio**
day/week/month/year	**iméra/evdomáda/mínas/ chrónos**
left/right	**aristerá/dexiá**
up/down	**epáno/káto**
good/bad	**kalós/kakós**
big/small	**megálos/mikrós**
cheap/expensive	**ftinós/akrivós**
hot/cold	**zestós/kríos**
old/new	**paliós/néos**
open/closed	**aniktós/klistós**
here/there	**edó/ekí**
free (vacant)/occupied	**eléftheri/kratiméni**
early/late	**norís/argá**
easy/difficult	**éfkolos/dískolos**
Does anybody here speak English?	**Milá kanís angliká?**
What does this mean?	**Ti siméni aftó?**
I don't understand.	**Den katalavéno.**
Please write it down.	**Parakaló grápste to.**
Is there an admission charge?	**Prépi na pliróso ísodo?**
Waiter, please!	**Garsóni (garçon), parakaló!**
I'd like ...	**Tha íthela ...**
How much is that?	**Póso káni aftó?**
Have you something less expensive?	**Échete káti ftinótero?**
What time is it?	**Ti óra íne?**
Just a minute.	**Éna leptó.**
Help me, please.	**Voithíste me, parakaló.**